The Barbary Wars

A Captivating Guide to the First Overseas Wars Conducted by the United States

Free Bonus from Captivating History (Available for a Limited time)

Hi History Lovers!

Now you have a chance to join our exclusive history list so you can get your first history ebook for free as well as discounts and a potential to get more history books for free! Simply visit the link below to join.

Captivatinghistory.com/ebook

Also, make sure to follow us on Facebook, Twitter and Youtube by searching for Captivating History.

Table of Contents

Introduction

After the United States gained independence, it lost the protection of the British Royal Navy, and American ships became vulnerable to pirate attacks. The most serious situation was that of American shipping bound for the Mediterranean, which saw a hundred ships a year travel to the region. Sometimes, these ships became the victims of the Muslim Barbary pirates based in North Africa. They mainly came from Algiers, Tunis, Tripoli, and a city in Morocco.

The young United States engaged in two wars, known as the Barbary Wars, with the Barbary pirate states. The first conflict was from 1801 to 1805 against Tripoli, and the second was against Algiers in 1815.

The conflict began when Americans had to ransom sailors captured by the corsairs and pay tribute to them to prevent attacks on American shipping. The story includes probably the greatest humiliation of any US Navy ship ever, as it was compelled to fly the Algerian flag and carry a hundred slaves, a harem, and a zoo from Algiers in North Africa to Istanbul, the Ottoman Empire's capital. The story of the wars also includes the disastrous loss of a frigate and one of the most heroic actions by any American in any war. It includes the bizarre march of an American force from Cairo for five hundred miles across the Libyan Desert, the first American invasion anywhere outside of North America, and the source of the line in the "Marines' Hymn," "From the Halls of Montezuma to the shores of Tripoli."

This captivating story begins when the United States was almost powerless to prevent attacks on its ships and ends with the US Navy becoming a significant and highly respected professional force capable of protecting the country.

Chapter 1 – Deys, Beys, and Bashaws

The world of the Barbary pirates was North Africa, sometimes called the Maghreb, a name that comes from an Arabic term referring to the setting sun because it was west of the classic Muslim world. In effect, it meant west of Egypt and included present-day Libya, Tunisia, Algeria, and Morocco.

The term "Barbary" has unclear origins but probably refers to the indigenous people of the Barbary Coast, the people called Berbers. An alternative etymology is the story that the classical Greeks thought that non-Greeks sounded crude when they talked, claiming that everything they said sounded like "Baa baa." It has been claimed that story is the origin of the word "barbarian."

The Barbary Coast was lightly populated and mostly desert, mountains, and rugged country, with some areas being well-watered and friendly to agriculture. The distance between the cities was considerable. It took four days to sail from Tangier at the Straits of Gibraltar to Algiers and another four or five more days to Tunis. Tripoli was four days' sail beyond that. Contrary winds and currents could reduce or extend the usual sailing times. An overland courier traveling by horse or camel might take twenty days to go from Algiers to Tripoli. The distance meant slow communications and that decisions had to be made on the information that was available.[1]

Historians, commentators, and contemporary descriptions and documents are often not very precise as to who was considered to be a Barbary pirate. The native peoples were various tribes of Berbers, and there was a mix of Arabs who came when Islam expanded across North Africa. People living in the Barbary cities of Algiers, Tunis, and Tripoli were a literal polyglot mix of Berbers, Arabs, Turks, Levantines (people from the Levant, the eastern coastal region of the Mediterranean), renegade Christians, captives held for ransom, and black and Christian slaves. The Barbary coast extended from Morocco to Algiers and on to Tunis and Tripoli, almost two thousand miles along the coast. Tripoli often controlled areas to the east.

During the Barbary pirates' wars with the US, they could be better described as Muslim privateers. "Corsairs" is a convenient word to describe them. Sometimes, they were pirates, plundering every ship they met. A privateer might be described as an official pirate licensed by some recognized state entity, whether a kingdom, nation, or city-state. Privateers were supposed to prey only on recognized enemies after a formal declaration of war. They might still attack ships without a formal declaration of war, like the famed English swashbucklers Thomas Hawkins and Sir Francis Drake. One difference between pirates and privateers is that pirates were usually hanged or drowned after being made prisoners, while privateers might be made prisoners of war. Privateers easily crossed the line into piracy.

The three Barbary Coast cities were sometimes used as havens for corsairs that came from Morocco, particularly those from Salé. After the mid-1500s, they were, in theory, dependencies of the Ottoman Empire and sometimes had a governor appointed by Istanbul, who acted as a kind of regent. Thus, the three cities are also sometimes called the "Regencies." The Ottomans' power never extended to Morocco, though.

A bit of history will help clarify how and why the Barbary States emerge. The American wars with the Barbary States occurred from 1801 to 1805 and then 1815 when the Barbary States were in decline but

[1] Daly, Robert. The Diplomatic Relations of the United States with the Barbary Coast, 1790-1801. Thesis, Loyola University, Chicago, IL., 1940
https://ecommons.luc.edu/cgi/viewcontent.cgi?referer=&httpsredir=1&article=1128&context=luc_theses. Pg. 1.

still dangerous. The pirate states were centered on the cities of Tripoli, Tunis, Algiers, and cities in Morocco. At the time of the two Barbary Wars, the ruler in Algiers was called a dey in English, the ruler in Tunis a bey, and the ruler in Tripoli a bashaw or pasha. "Bey" comes from the Turkish beg, which means a leader, and "dey" may be a corruption of it. "Bashaw" is a version of the Turkish pasha, meaning chief.

There was a strong religious element in the early days of the Barbary corsairs. It was almost like a holy war, or jihad, a sense of righteous fighting against Christians. There were some Christian corsairs, particularly the Knights of Malta, who raided Muslim shipping for centuries, although they had faded into insignificance by the time Americans made war on the Barbary coast.

The Maghreb region has a complicated history. It was ruled by Phoenicians, Greeks, Carthaginians, Romans, Byzantines, Vandals, Umayyads, Mamluks, local dynasties, and Ottoman Turks. A persistent element was warfare between states in North Africa and southern Europe and tensions between the coastal cities and the rural interior.

The most dangerous rival to ancient Rome was the city of Carthage, located not far from where Tunis is today. Carthage controlled much of North Africa, many of the Mediterranean islands, and much of Spain. The Romans defeated the Carthaginians in a series of wars that included the famed Hannibal Barca, probably Rome's most dangerous enemy. Hannibal was the leader who famously brought war elephants across the Alps into Italy.

Rome and Carthage fought some of the largest naval battles in history. The battle off Cape Ecnomus in 256 BCE is thought to have involved nearly 300,000 men, including soldiers, crewmen, and galley slaves. The Romans suffered ten thousand deaths, and the Carthaginians suffered thirty thousand or more. The Romans destroyed Carthage in 146 BCE. The pattern of fighting at sea between Europeans and North Africans lasted two thousand years.

Roman North Africa eventually fell to the Germanic Vandals in 429 CE. The Vandals crossed into Africa from Spain and took over most of Roman North Africa. The Vandals exchanged their horses for ships and became formidable pirates. Like the later Barbary corsairs, the Vandals raided the coasts of Spain, Gaul (France), the Mediterranean islands, and Italy, and their highly destructive plundering tendencies gave English the word "vandal."

The Vandals were taken out by the Byzantines in 533 CE, who briefly established control of much of former Roman Africa. They were thrown out of the Maghreb by the Muslims in the late 7th century CE. The Muslims marched west out of Egypt, but it took them decades to finalize their conquest, with it being finished around 682 CE when all of North Africa and most of Spain and Portugal fell to the Muslims. The Berber peoples offered stubborn resistance to the Arab invasions, and even after converting to Islam, they preferred autonomy. The Umayyad Caliphate (661–750), based in Damascus, Syria, made the Maghreb part of an immense Islamic empire that extended far into central Asia and the borders of India.

The Umayyads fell to the Abbasid Caliphate, based in Baghdad, Iraq, which ruled much of the Muslim world from 750 to 1258. "Caliph" was the title given to men who were regarded as the successors of the Prophet Muhammad. They were widely seen as the legitimate leaders of Islam. The title belonged to the Umayyads, then the Abbasids, then the Mamluks in Egypt, and finally the Ottomans in Istanbul until they fell in 1918. Ataturk, an Ottoman general who was the architect of modern Turkey, abolished the office in 1924. A branch of the Umayyads fled from the Middle East and established a dynasty based at Córdoba in Spain, with North Africa sometimes functioning as a zone of conflict between the dynasties.

The Mamluks took power in Egypt in 1250 and ruled until the Ottomans conquered Egypt in 1517. The Mamluks were slave soldiers who had been recruited from the Caucasus region of the Black Sea. They are often called Circassians, although they came from a number of Caucasian peoples. The slave soldiers became powerful and eventually replaced their masters as rulers of Egypt. The Mamluks ruled much of the Maghreb, as well as Palestine and Syria. They remained powerful even after their subjugation to the Ottomans. Mamluk history shows that slaves in the Islamic world could achieve freedom and become powerful. Several of the most famous Barbary corsairs had been enslaved and managed to become the leaders of large and powerful fleets.

In the Maghreb, there were also a number of local dynasties of Berber and Arab origin, which contested with each other and with outsiders for power. While Moroccan history overlaps some of the Maghreb's history, its history is largely separate. There were dynasties called the Almoravids (1062–1150) and Almohads (1150–1269) that combined Morocco, parts of North Africa, Spain, and some of the Sahel (the region between the Sahara and the forested regions to the south). These two dynasties originated as puritanical reformist movements within Islam from visionary prophets deep in the Sahel who attracted vast numbers of followers bent on conquering and purifying Islam. These dynasties also had corsairs raiding Christian enemies, and when the dynasties broke down, the corsairs sometimes became pirates due to the chaos that ensued.

Long before the Barbary States took their final form in the 16th century, Muslim corsairs captured Christian ships, held Christians for ransom, and plundered coastal communities along the European coasts. In the 13th century, Pope Innocent III agreed to the founding of a new religious order called the Society of the Fathers of the Redemption, which was dedicated to ransoming Christians from Muslim captivity. Other religious orders were founded for the same cause, and their efforts continued for centuries.

These clerics dedicated their lives to ransoming captives and bringing them home. Some even traveled to Muslim lands to try to ease the conditions the slaves were facing. They were particularly concerned with preventing Christians from converting to Islam. Sending money to the orders that ransomed captives was seen as a very Christian thing to do. Obtaining ransom seems to have produced as good an income as selling captives in the slave markets.[2]

The Barbary Coast was more than just Muslim corsairs plundering Europe. Just as the Muslim corsairs had an element of a jihad (holy war) when they attacked Christian shipping and coasts, there were Christian corsairs waging something like a holy war against Islam. The most notable group was the Knights Hospitaller. It was formed in Jerusalem during the Crusades to fight against Muslim attacks and to protect pilgrims. It was a military order of knights dedicated to defending Catholicism. Defending Christianity included capturing Muslim ships, enslaving Muslim captives, and sometimes occupying and holding ports and fortresses.

When the Christian states in the Holy Land fell in the 13th century, the Knights Hospitaller retreated to Cyprus and then to the island of Rhodes off the south coast of Anatolia. Like the Vandals, they gave up

---

[2] Daly, Robert. The Diplomatic Relations of the United States with the Barbary Coast, 1790-1801. Pg. 4.

their horses for ships. From Rhodes, they raided Muslim coasts and shipping for a couple of centuries until an Ottoman attack ousted them. Their resistance to the Ottoman invasion of Rhodes was so fierce that the sultan allowed them to leave. They moved on to Malta in 1522 and continued depredations against the Muslims. Christian corsairs from Malta fought Muslim corsairs from Barbary, but both faded in the 18th century, with the knights reaching near insignificance. Napoleon put an end to the Knights Hospitaller on his way to invade Egypt.[3]

Both Christian and Muslim corsairs used similar ships. They often used galleys, a form of ship going back to classical times. They were long and narrow and rowed by volunteers or, more often, slaves. The galleys tended to only have a couple of cannons because they were lightly built. The vibrations caused by a cannonade might shake a galley to pieces. Severe shaking could loosen the planking of the hull and literally sink a galley. Galleys and sailing ships had large crews because the most common tactic was to close on a merchant ship and board it, overwhelming the other crew and putting a prize crew on board to sail the captured ship to the corsair's base.

Early on, the ships had triangular sail rigs (called lateen rigs) and were not particularly large, but they did sail fast. Preying on merchant ships did not require heavy armament because such ships tended to have small crews. Corsairs were generally not interested in slugging it out with warships, which tended to have large crews trained in battle and equipped with heavy armament. Later, with the development of new ship types like the caravel, Barbary pirates began to use these vessels, particularly for raiding the Atlantic.

The best sailing in the Mediterranean is from April to October. Winter could bring gales that made sailing dangerous, and storms could be destructive. Galleys were more vulnerable to wind and waves than sturdier-built sailing ships. Even with sailing ships, prudent commanders campaigned in favorable seasons and paid close attention to the weather. Even though tides were far lower in the Mediterranean than in the Atlantic and the waves not as vast, storms could be dangerous and sink entire fleets.

---

[3] Jamieson, Alan. *Lords of the Sea. A History of the Barbary Corsairs.* London: Reaktion Books, 2012.

As the modern sailing ship was developed in the 15th century in Europe, the square sail rigs typical of ships sailing on the rougher waters of the Atlantic merged with the Mediterranean triangular sail rigs, gradually producing the fast and maneuverable warship called the caravel. It is no coincidence that the main developers of this ship were the Portuguese, whose ships frequented both the Mediterranean and Africa's Atlantic coast.

The caravels were built in a more robust manner and could carry more cargo and much more artillery than galleys. The caravels were the primary ships used in the early Iberian voyages of discovery and were the ancestors of the much larger ships that carried scores of cannons and crews of a thousand.

The Barbary States were quick to adapt their fleets to incorporate these developing forms of shipping and hired European shipwrights to build them. Galleys remained the most important kind of warship in the Mediterranean until the later 16th century and continued to be used into the 19th century. Galleys had advantages that kept them useful. They were not dependent on the wind, performed well in enclosed bays, had shallower drafts, and were highly maneuverable.

Throughout this welter of conquerors and dynasties, three cities always remained important: Algiers, Tunis, and Tripoli. Local dynasties were sometimes based in the cities, and sometimes, they were ruled by viceroys of empires. The relationships between the cities and their hinterlands tended to be troubled. At times, the cities controlled a large hinterland. Near the end of the Barbary period, Algiers controlled much of the coast and part of the interior of Algeria, Tunis came to control much of what is now Tunisia, and Tripoli controlled the coasts and part of the interior of Cyrenaica, what is now northeast Libya and east as far as Derna into the Libyan Desert. The interior Arab and Berber clans were often fractious, and it took a formidable leader to assert effective control.

These cities were also the northern terminals of trade routes from deep in Africa, which crossed the Sahara. The trade went back many centuries, probably before the Romans and Carthaginians. The trade involved salt, ivory, gold, slaves, weapons, and other high-value items.

The Barbary States began to take their modern form because of the Ottoman Turkish conquest of Byzantium in 1453, which marked the emergence of the Ottomans as the major Muslim power in the Middle

East, the Balkans in Europe, and the Mediterranean. The Ottomans defeated the Mamluk sultanate in 1517, meaning the Ottomans were now in control of the western ends of the trade routes into Asia that ultimately went to India and China. This disrupted trade was one of the reasons Portugal began its circumnavigation of Africa (the Portuguese first rounded the Cape of Good Hope at the southern tip of Africa in 1488), which began Portugal's Indian Ocean empire.

It also marked the emergence of the Ottomans as a major threat to Europe. They controlled Greece and most of the Balkans for four hundred years, Hungary for almost two centuries, and sometimes controlled portions of Ukraine and Russia. The Black Sea remained an Ottoman "lake" until the capture of Crimea by Russia in 1783. The Ottomans retained much of their European empire until the Balkan Wars of 1912. They were a major influence on the Barbary Coast until the Italians took Tripoli in 1911.

As the Ottomans were consolidating their empire, Spain was extinguishing the last Muslim kingdoms in Spain, conquering Granada in 1492. This had a major effect on the Maghreb, as tens of thousands of Muslim refugees left for Morocco, Algiers, and other friendly places. Spain also expelled its sizable Jewish community in 1492, which found ready refuge on the Barbary Coast and in the Ottoman realm.

Many Muslims remained in Spain and were forced to convert to Catholicism. These groups were called Moriscos, but they were suspected of being Muslim spies and agents. The Moriscos were persecuted and were sometimes victims of the Inquisition. They apparently did sometimes aid Barbary, Ottoman, and Moroccan ships raiding the Spanish coast, so they, too, were expelled from 1609 to 1614. Several hundred thousand Moriscos were expelled, and they found refuge in Morocco and the Maghreb. They had an abiding hatred for the Spanish, and their familiarity with Spanish waters was helpful to corsairs raiding there.

Spain gradually developed an American empire after 1492, and in the 16th century, spectacularly rich sources of silver were discovered in Mexico and Peru. The silver fueled Spain's rise to becoming the greatest power in Europe in the 1500s and paid for the long wars between the Spanish and the Turks. American silver fueled Spain's wars against the rise of Protestantism in Europe and helped fuel the Austrian Habsburg wars in the Balkans against the Ottomans. Wealth coming from Spain's

American empire financed the ongoing Spanish and Portuguese wars against Islam. And it financed Spanish campaigns against the Barbary Coast.

After ousting Islam from Iberia, the Spanish attacked North Africa as far east as Egypt. Spain took control of a number of fortifiable places along the North African coast, including Algiers. The Portuguese took control of several strong points along Morocco's Atlantic coast. These Spanish and Portuguese enclaves changed hands several times. Spain still possesses the Ceuta and Melilla enclaves in North Africa five hundred years later.

The two most crucial personalities in the several centuries of Barbary Coast history were two brothers, Aruj (also known as Oruc Reis) and Hizir. Their last name was Barbarossa because of their red beards. They were sons of a retired Turkish sipahi (professional cavalryman) who had settled on the Greek island of Lesbos. Some historians claim that their father was a Greek who converted to Islam. Their father became a trader, and two of his sons were on board an Ottoman ship when it was taken by a corsair of the Knights of St. John. One brother was killed (Hizir was not on board), and Aruj spent three years as a galley slave until he escaped.[4]

Aruj Barbarossa and his brother Hizir began their careers as corsair captains. They were first based at Antalya on the southern coast of Anatolia. Both brothers were charismatic and ruthless, with a talent for leadership. From Anatolia, they moved to the island of Djerba off the Tunisian coast. They were spectacularly successful and attracted a powerful group of followers. Led by Aruj, they had sufficient numbers of ships to try to take Algiers in 1513 and 1515. They finally took the city in 1516, capturing it from the Spanish. The Spanish tried to recover it, and Aruj was killed fighting them.

In 1519, Hizir appealed to the Ottomans in Istanbul for help against the Spanish. Istanbul responded by sending two thousand Janissaries and a fleet of ships. The Janissaries were professional infantry whose origin lay in a tax that took boys from Christian families in parts of the Balkans. They were converted to Islam and trained as administrators and soldiers. As slaves, they owed loyalty only to the Ottoman sultan, not to

---

[4] Tinniswood, Adrian. *Pirates of Barbary*, New York: Riverhead Books, 2010. Google Books access April 13, 2023.

descendants of regional dynasties the Ottomans had conquered, so they were considered exceptionally loyal. With Ottoman support, Algiers remained in the possession of Barbarossa. Algiers had eighteen galleys by 1529 and was raiding Spain, Sicily, and Calabria.[5]

Ottoman assistance tilted the balance of power, and Spain barely held on to a few of its North African outposts. Hizir was invited to Istanbul by Sultan Suleiman the Magnificent (the conqueror of Egypt) and was appointed kapudan pasha, commander (or grand admiral) of the Ottoman navy. He was given the honorary name of Khair ad-Din and was also known as Hayreddin Barbarossa. He proved to be one of the best Ottoman naval commanders in history. He captured Tunis in 1534 and had 110 galleys under his command in the early 1540s. He defeated a Christian fleet sent by Charles V (who ruled Spain and the Holy Roman Empire). Charles V's fleet was commanded by the equally formidable Genoese commander Andrea Doria in the Battle of Preveza in 1538.[6]

Khair ad-Din was commander of the Ottoman fleet in one of the most peculiar situations in European history. Francis I of France was at war with Charles V of Spain and the Holy Roman Empire over territories in Italy. Francis requested an alliance with the Ottomans, and the Ottomans agreed. The Ottoman fleet helped the French capture Nice and then Savoy. The Ottoman fleet spent the winter of 1543/44 in the French port of Toulon, not far from Marseilles. A large Muslim fleet staying the winter at a Christian port scandalized Europe, as a Christian king was the host and ally of a Muslim pirate commanding the sultan's navy.[7]

Khair ad-Din retired to Istanbul in 1546 in his late sixties, an old age for a corsair captain. His former commanders remained active in the wars with the Spanish. Tunis and Tripoli changed hands but were finally wrested from the Spanish (Tripoli in 1551 and Tunis again in 1574). Tripoli was taken from the Knights of Malta, who were supported by Spain. Another powerful and highly successful corsair, Dragut, who had been one of Khair ad-Din's commanders, was appointed governor of Tripoli by Suleiman. Dragut lived to be eighty years old, a very old age

[5] Tinniswood, Adrian. *Pirates of Barbary.*

[6] Jamieson, Alan. *Lords of the Sea. A History of the Barbary Corsairs.* Pg. 24.

[7] Tinniswood, Adrian. *Pirates of Barbary.*

for a corsair leader, and he led raids well into his old age.

As mentioned, Charles V was king of Spain from 1516 to 1556 and the Holy Roman emperor from 1519 to 1556, making him the most powerful man in Europe, except possibly for Ottoman Sultan Suleiman the Great (r. 1520–1556). Charles considered himself the leader of Christendom and the chief defender against the Ottomans. American silver allowed Spain to become the most powerful kingdom in Europe and fueled Charles V's wars. Spain ruled in Iberia, as well as Sardinia, Sicily, Naples, and southern Italy. Charles V also inherited vast lands in central Europe.

In 1535, Charles organized a massive strike against Tunis and imposed a settlement on the city, including a Spanish garrison nearby. Perhaps twenty thousand Christian prisoners were freed. In 1541, Charles struck at Tripoli, forcing the bey to come to terms. The bey agreed to release Christian prisoners and no longer attack Spanish ships.[8]

In 1541, he assembled a huge force to invade Algiers, consisting of sixty-five galleys and four hundred transport ships manned by twelve thousand sailors and twenty-four soldiers. The soldiers were mostly German, Spanish, and Italian. One of them was Hernán Cortés, who had conquered the Aztecs in Mexico.

The force landed near Algiers and intended to conquer it. The Ottoman commander was Hassan, a Sardinian who had turned Turk. Hassan had only about six thousand soldiers, but he had the advantage of luck. On October 26th, 1541, a savage storm struck and sank 150 of the emperor's ships. Charles V seems to simply have given up and ordered the remainder of his force back on ships to go home. Some two thousand horses were tossed overboard to make room for the soldiers on the remaining ships. The Christian force lost about eight thousand men, and four thousand were captured. These men were soon sold in the slave markets. So many slaves were available that, for a time, the price declined sharply.[9]

The emperor's campaign against Algiers was probably the largest land campaign in the Barbary region until the French invaded Algeria in 1830. It was probably equaled by the disastrous Portuguese invasion of

---

[8] Daly, Robert. The Diplomatic Relations of the United States with the Barbary Coast, 1790-1801. Pg. 61.

[9] Jamieson, Alan. *Lords of the Sea. A History of the Barbary Corsairs.* Pg. 24-27.

Morocco in 1578.

The connections between Istanbul and the Barbary States were sporadic, and Istanbul's actual control was rare. Over time, the Ottoman soldiers and administrators who came to the Barbary Coast married into local families, founding groups called Kouloughlis. By the 1700s, their descendants formed hereditary dynasties in Tunis and Tripoli.[10]

Dynastic affairs in Europe also affected the Barbary Coast. Charles V retired in 1556, splitting his empire into Spain and its territories under his son Philip II and the Austrian and central European lands of the Holy Roman Empire to his brother Ferdinand. This split the Habsburgs into a Spanish branch in Madrid and an Austrian branch in Vienna. Spain became the primary enemy of the corsairs and the Ottomans at sea, and the Austrians became the main enemy of the Ottomans on land in Europe. Not long after, Portugal, which had been enriched by its trade with India, invaded Morocco with the hope of conquering it but was disastrously defeated at the Battle of the Three Kings. Portugal was left leaderless and was incorporated into Spain in 1580. Spain ruled Flanders (what is now Belgium and the Netherlands), vast areas in the Americas, and the Philippines in Asia.

There's a literary footnote to all this. Miguel de Cervantes, author of Don Quixote and one of the greatest Spanish writers, was captured by Barbary corsairs and held as a prisoner from 1575 to 1580. He became a galley slave. He was ransomed by the Trinitarians, a Catholic order focusing on rescuing Christians from Muslim captivity. Perhaps Quixote's tilting at windmills in the novel was in some way related to Spain's many abortive efforts to defeat and control the Barbary States.

In one huge event, the Barbary corsairs from Algiers were extremely important. The massive and exceedingly bloody naval Battle of Lepanto was fought on October 7th, 1571, off the shores of Greece. The battle pitted naval forces from Spain, Venice, the pope, Genoa, and the Knights of Malta against the Turks. The Ottomans had invaded the Venetian possession of Cyprus, and the Venetians asked the pope for help in fighting off the Turks. It took time to assemble, but a Christian alliance was formed that put more than two hundred galleys to sea, along with several of the new galleasses devised by Venice. The galleasses were very large galleys that were built much more sturdily and featured more

---

[10] Meredith, Martin. *The Futures of Africa.* New York: Public Affairs, 2014. Pg. 150.

artillery than a galley. The fleet was commanded by Don Juan of Austria, the illegitimate brother of Charles V, and by another Andrea Doria of the great Genoese family of naval commanders.

The Christian fleet found the Ottoman fleet just off the Greek coast. It, too, was comprised of more than two hundred galleys and was commanded by an Ottoman admiral, with one wing commanded by Uluj Ali, Dey of Algiers. These fleets were huge, with roughly forty-five thousand sailors and soldiers in each fleet. Some of the fighting was not so different from ancient Roman and Carthaginian days, with swordsmen boarding enemy ships and bowmen shooting arrows. At Lepanto, both sides used musketeers, and each side had more than a thousand cannons, although the Christian side had more. The Ottoman Janissaries were balanced by veterans of the famed Spanish Tercios, with both groups functioning as marines.

The result was a decisive Christian victory. The Ottomans lost around two hundred ships sunk or captured, and the alliance suffered several dozen. The casualties were enormous, with the Christian side suffering seven thousand or more killed. The Turks lost even more men, but it is unknown how many; perhaps twenty thousand were killed. An estimated ten thousand Christian galley slaves were freed, and several thousand on the Turkish side were captured, destined to become galley slaves on Christian ships.

The only Ottoman commander to have any success at Lepanto was Uluj Ali, the dey of Algiers. He escaped the battle and sailed to Istanbul with seventy or eighty surviving ships. The Turks still captured Cyprus and, by the next year, had built enough ships to replace the huge losses at the battle. Uluj Ali (also known as Occhiali) continued raiding and achieved such fame that his name inspired terror. He lived an extraordinarily long life for a naval commander in the 16th century, living from 1500 to 1587. Remarkably, Uluj Ali was Italian. He had been captured by a Barbary corsair when he was seventeen. He served as a galley slave and then converted to Islam. Uluj Ali died in Istanbul as a very old, very rich, and very powerful man.

Following the Battle of Lepanto, the Turks continued to dominate the eastern half of the Mediterranean, and Spain dominated the western half of the sea. The Barbary corsairs remained active and formidable in the western half, at times extending out into the Atlantic. Italy was not united, and France was suffering devastating wars of religion between

Catholics and Protestants.

The Barbary Coast cities were at their most formidable between about 1550 and 1730. The corsairs were the principal factor in the economies of the Barbary cities, and slaves were the most valuable booty because they could be bought and sold. If the captives were rich or lucky, they might be ransomed, making ransom money very important to the Barbary economies.

At first, the Barbary cities were governed by Ottoman representatives. Initially, the Porte (a term for the sultan's government) appointed governors for three-year terms. "Governors" had considerable power but were not dictatorial; they had councils made up of local leaders, so in effect, it was a kind of co-rule between the Ottoman appointee and influential local leaders. Istanbul auctioned off the governorship to the highest bidder.[11]

While the numbers are highly controversial, the most common estimate of captives taken from European shipping and from raids on European coasts from 1550 to 1730 is a million. During most of that span, Algiers alone usually had around twenty-five thousand Christian captives, with considerably smaller numbers in Tripoli and Tunis. The Barbary cities also were refuges for hundreds of European pirates, many of whom converted to Islam.[12]

This "white slave trade" was contemporaneous with the Atlantic slave trade, although it was considerably smaller. The peak of the Atlantic slave trade was in the 1700s, and historians estimate that, overall, the Atlantic slave trade took about eleven million Africans to the Americas, with another million or so dying during the crossing. Slaves in the Atlantic trade had no option of being ransomed or achieving some equality by turning Muslim.

The corsairs were adept at slipping into harbors and coasts, evading defenses, and spreading terror wherever they went. Several corsairs in a coordinated raid could land scores or even hundreds of armed men to loot communities and round up captives. They struck quickly and were

---

[11] Wilson, Gary. *American Prisoners in the Barbary Nations, 1784-1816.* Dissertation, North Texas State University, 1979.
https://digital.library.unt.edu/ark:/67531/metadc331824/m2/1/high_res_d/1002783548-Wilson.pdf. Pgs. 3-4.

[12] Meredith, Martin. *The Futures of Africa*, Pg. 151.

usually gone before defenders could respond. Corsairs did most of their depredations within the Mediterranean, but they sometimes raided the Atlantic. The raids into the Atlantic reached as far as Iceland, Scotland, and Scandinavia, and those raids were often led by European renegades who had "turned Turk," which means they had converted to Islam. The renegades were familiar with northern waters and knew where vulnerable regions were. These far-ranging corsairs caused panic, although they were episodes rather than the long-lasting depredations against the Mediterranean coasts of Spain, France, and Italy.

Two of the most infamous incidents of Barbary raids involving Iceland happened in 1627. The first raiders were from Salé, Morocco. They raided Iceland in June and carried away several dozen captives. They were led by a Dutchman who had turned Turk named Murat Reis ("reis" means captain). His Dutch name had been Janszoon van Haarlem. Another and much more deadly raid was by Algerian corsairs, who struck in early July and stayed in Icelandic waters for more than a week. They, too, were led by a renegade Dutchman. History relays that his name was Murad. The Algerians burned several settlements and carried off about four hundred people.[13]

Waters that far north would have been strange and unfamiliar to sailors used to the calmer Mediterranean. The knowledge of the European renegades made these far-flung raids possible. The Icelanders were sold in the usual slave markets. One of the captives was let go to plead for help in Denmark (Iceland was Danish then), with the captors hoping for ransom payments. A decade after their capture, about thirty were ransomed, and twenty-seven of the original four hundred captives made it back to Iceland.[14]

There were other Barbary raids that happened outside of the Mediterranean. In August 1625, corsairs struck Mount's Bay in Cornwall, carrying off sixty English men, women, and children. Other raids reached Scotland. In 1631, Algerian corsairs raided the community of Baltimore in Ireland, taking more than a hundred people captive. The corsair captain seems to have been the same renegade Dutchman that led an earlier raid on Iceland.

---

[13] Davies, J.D. "The Barbary Corsair Raid on Iceland, 1627." Blog.
https://jddavies.com/2017/02/20/the-barbary-corsair-raid-on-iceland-1627/
[14] Davies, J.D. "The Barbary Corsair Raid on Iceland, 1627."

In 1640, it was estimated that there were some three thousand English captives in Algiers. Charities were set up to raise money for ransoms, and fishing villages pooled money to ransom captive fishermen, which might be called a kind of pirate insurance.[15]

Other places set up funds to ransom captives. Hamburg and Lübeck, the major powers in the merchant German Hanseatic Union in the Baltic Sea region, financed a fund called the Sklavenkasse from a tax on shipping so there would be money for ransoms. Swedish sailors had a small amount deducted from their pay to set up funds for ransoming captured sailors.[16]

Those three thousand English captives in Algiers would have come from a combination of taking fishing boats and merchant ships at sea and raids on coastal communities. Oliver Cromwell, the formidable Lord Protector of England following the English Civil War, ordered captured pirates, including Barbary pirates, to be slowly drowned. The English (England did not become Britain until 1707 when England and Scotland merged) sometimes reacted with force and struck back. In 1675, a Royal Navy squadron ventured into the Mediterranean and bombarded Tripoli, which helped generate a peace settlement for a time.

Captives were not always made slaves. Important captives might be held in a kind of house arrest, awaiting ransom. Many of the actual slaves in the Barbary States were black slaves who came from south of the Sahara as part of a long-established trade network. European captives were enslaved, but for some, it was only for months or a few years before they were ransomed. Ransoms and protection money provided steady income, as did loot, and slaves brought from below the Sahara more often engaged in physical labor than European slaves. The slaves from the south did not have families or religious orders to ransom them; their only recourse to lighten their burden was to convert to Islam. There were also slaves from elsewhere in the Ottoman Empire, including Georgians and Circassians from the Caucasus.[17]

[15] Johnson, Ben. "Barbary Pirates and English Slaves." History UK. Retrieved April 11, 2023. https://www.historic-uk.com/HistoryUK/HistoryofEngland/Barbary-Pirates-English-Slaves/

[16] Sutton, Angela. *White Slaves in Barbary: The Early American Republic, Orientalism and the Barbary Pirates.* Thesis, Vanderbilt University, Nashville, TN, 2009. Retrieved April 10, 2023. https://ir.vanderbilt.edu/xmlui/bitstream/handle/1803/14312/SuttonWhiteSlaves.pdf?sequence=1&isAllowed=y. Pg. 9.

[17] Sutton, Angela. *White Slaves in Barbary: The Early American Republic, Orientalism and the*

As time went on, the relative power of the corsair captains and the city rulers changed. Some of this seems to be due to the professional Janissaries, which gave the Ottoman regents an army to force obedience on the people they oversaw. The bey, dey, and pasha gained more power over their cities and hinterlands, and the power of the corsair captains waned. The net impact was that the pirates became corsairs and more like a slave-raiding navy than a nest of pirates.[18]

One artifact of the slave-raiding corsairs still remains. Southern Italy, Sicily, and a few other places were so affected by the raids over the generations that communities abandoned the coasts and moved into the interior into fortified villages in the hills. Those places today are picturesque tourist attractions and are often noted for their colorful architecture and evocation of past centuries. What modern tourism sees as colorful and quaint was once deadly serious, as it was once an effort to protect people from slave raiders.

Slavery went both ways. Thousands of Muslims were captured in European and Knights of Malta raids. During King Louis XIV's reign (r. 1643-1715), the French Navy still used many galleys in the Mediterranean and had twelve thousand slaves rowing them. About a quarter of those were Turks and Maghrebians.[19]

Thus, Christians and Muslims continued to raid each other, although the 1500s was the peak. Both Spain and the Ottoman Empire declined in power during the 1600s. Morocco fragmented over a dynastic quarrel. Spain and Portugal retained a few posts on the Atlantic and North African coasts, including Ma'amur and Mazagar in Morocco, as well as Tangier, Ceuta, Oran, and Melilla. The Barbary cities were nominally governed by Ottoman regents but had local autonomy.[20]

Barbary Pirates. Pg. 12.

[18] Monsieurs, Roel. *The Causes and Consequences of the First Barbary War 1801-1805.* Thesis, July 2016. Erasmus University, Rotterdam, NE. Retrieved April 9, 2023. https://thesis.eur.nl/pub/34940. Pg. 35.

[19] Ribiero, Jorge Martins. "Conflict and Peace in the Mediterranean: Barbary Privateering in the Late 18th and Early 19th Centuries." 159-179 in D'Angelo and Ribiero, Editors, *Borders and Conflicts in the Mediterranean.* Fisciano, Italy 2016. Retrieved April 13, 2023. https://repositorio-aberto.up.pt/bitstream/10216/86826/2/163741.pdf. Pg. 161.

[20] Tinniswood, Adrian. *Pirates of Barbary.*

While the corsairs probably raided European coasts much more often than Europeans raided the Barbary Coast, Europeans attacked often enough to require stout defenses. Between 1610 and 1621 alone, attacks came from Malta, Spain, Sicily, Tuscany, France, England, and the Netherlands. Some of these raids took hundreds, even thousands, of Maghrebians prisoners.[21]

The corsairs continued to attract European renegades. The war between England and Spain, which included the famous Spanish Armada of 1588, lasted from 1585 to 1605. When it ended, a significant number of privateers became unemployed. Some turned pirate, and some of them joined the Barbary corsairs, converting to Islam. It is unknown if any sailors from the Barbary region joined in the classic era of pirates in the Caribbean and Indian Ocean that lasted from about 1650 to the early 1700s

Europeans sometimes mounted campaigns against the Barbary Coast with the intention of conquering it. Aside from the attacks mounted by Charles V, Portugal mounted a massive invasion of Morocco in 1578, which was a catastrophic loss and left Portugal leaderless. In 1683, a large French fleet bombarded Algiers, reportedly killing thousands of people. A macabre story that seems to be true is that the enraged Algerians loaded their own cannons with twenty-one Frenchmen and fired them back at the French fleet. In 1688, another French fleet attacked, and the French consul was loaded into a cannon and fired at the attackers.[22]

The British became a permanent factor in the region by capturing Gibraltar from Spain in 1704. Gibraltar remained a British fortress and naval base for centuries. Gibraltar was also a fairly friendly place for American warships after the War of 1812. US Navy ships often anchored there during the Barbary Wars.

Two centuries later, in 1775, a large Spanish invasion force sailed for Morocco. The fleet totaled sixty-seven warships, including seven ships of the line and four hundred transports, manned by perhaps nineteen thousand sailors. However, Spain again suffered defeat.

---

[21] Wilson, Gary. *American Prisoners in the Barbary Nations, 1784-1816.* Pg. 10.

[22] Daly, Robert. The Diplomatic Relations of the United States with the Barbary Coast, 1790-1801. Pgs. 7-8.

The corsairs became slowly less significant in the late 1600s when Europe's main naval powers, the British, French, and Dutch, forced them to come to terms. The smaller and less powerful states, like Denmark, Sweden, the Kingdom of the Two Sicilies (Naples and southern Italy; Italy did not unify until 1861), and, a century later, the United States, continued to be prey. The three main Barbary cities also increasingly developed control of their hinterlands, which were largely populated by Berber tribes, some farmers, and some nomadic herders.

Chapter 2 – Independence, Piracy, and Tribute (1784–1800)

Ships from the English colonies in North America began sailing to Europe and the Mediterranean not long after they settled in the Americas. New England, in particular, had stony ground for farms, a burgeoning population, and good harbors, so making a living from the sea was a logical development. Ships sailed from Boston, New York, Philadelphia, Charleston, and elsewhere, carrying American products to the Caribbean and Europe. American ships were extensively involved in fishing. The American colonists came to dominate whaling and engaged in a wide variety of trades.

Barbary pirates were not a threat to much of this fast-growing merchant trade. The trade varied considerably; masts cut for the Royal Navy might go to Britain, or food products were shipped to the sugar islands in the West Indies to feed slaves. By the late period of British rule, colonial shipping was developing markets in Spain, Italy, and elsewhere in the Mediterranean. The corsairs were dangerous in the Mediterranean and the Atlantic off the coast of northwest Africa. The colonists' developing trade in the region meant that the threat from corsairs was also developing.

There were some incidents. The first ship sailing from the English colonies to be taken by a corsair was an English ship returning to England from the Salem settlement in Massachusetts. It was taken by a Moroccan corsair from Salé in 1625. Other English ships captured by corsairs probably had Americans on board.[23]

The plight of Americans captured by Barbary corsairs drew considerable public attention in the US, far more than the relatively small number of captives should have generated. Some of the public interest originated from the media of the day. The literary genre called "captivity narratives" had been popular for a century in both Britain and America, originating as stories and autobiographical accounts of English settlers who were held captive by the Native Americans and the French. Stories about captivity in New France often centered on a Protestant captive's resistance to attempts to convert to Roman Catholicism.

Accounts of being prisoners in the Barbary States went back to the 1600s in Britain and included accounts of several corsair raids in England itself. In the 1780s, the captivity narratives in the US included pamphlets and books about American sailors who experienced captivity in the Barbary States. Some of them centered on efforts to convert Christians to Islam. And just like some New Englanders converted to Catholicism and remained in Canada, some sailors turned Muslim and remained in North Africa.[24]

There was an undercurrent in these captivity narratives that one never referred to except indirectly. It was a prudish age for print, but there was an interest in the sexual aspect of captivity. The captivity narratives from the colonial wars with the Native Americans tiptoe around what might have happened to women who were taken prisoner. As far as scholars know, no American women were ever captured by Barbary corsairs, but there is evidence that the public thought that male captives could be subject to rape, which would have been met with outrage. The public's intense interest in redeeming prisoners may reflect such anxiety.

Colonists taken as prisoners aroused public sympathy. In 1700, the story of five New Yorkers languishing in servitude became a cause to get behind, perhaps due to newspaper accounts. The five had been captured in 1693. The governor pitched in, and churches collected donations. Many people contributed to the cause, and eventually, two of the five were ransomed. What happened to the other three is not known. Some of the funds left over from this were used in the construction of Trinity

[23] Wilson, Gary. *American Prisoners in the Barbary Nations, 1784-1816.* Pg. 18.

[24] Baepler, Paul. "White Slaves, African Masters." *Annals of the American Association of Political and Social Science.* Vol. 588, July 2003. 90-111. JSTOR access, April 11, 2023. Pg. 91.

Church in Manhattan.[25]

A peculiar dynamic of the Barbary slave narratives was the focus on white people being the slaves of Africans, which was widely seen as the reverse of American slavery. There must have been some African American sailors captured by the corsairs because free black men were often members of navy and merchant ship crews.

It is very likely that the popularity of the Barbary slave narratives had a considerable role in shaping how the American public felt about the Barbary Wars. The young United States had one of the highest literacy rates in the world. Newspapers were widespread and eagerly reprinted stories of adventure, and the government subsidized the post office, so books, pamphlets, and newspapers circulated even in rural areas.

Barbary slaves were the theme of more than just captivity narratives. Rumors sometimes swept through towns. In one case, a fake letter, ostensibly from the dey of Algiers, was widely reprinted; the letter demanded £100,000 and forty beautiful girls aged between twelve and eighteen. If this payment was not received, corsairs would burn Philadelphia to ashes. Some of the public believed it, and panic spread. This letter might have been someone's attempt at satire.[26]

In 1787, a political novel appeared by a man named Peter Markoe titled *The Algerian Spy in Pennsylvania*. The plot involved a spy named Mehmet connecting with Shay's Rebellion in Massachusetts and conspiring with authorities in Rhode Island to turn the state into an Algerian corsair base for devastating the American coast. Shay's Rebellion was a real event that lasted from 1786 to 1787, and Rhode Island was slow to ratify the Constitution, not doing so until 1790. The novel about a Barbary spy was partly propaganda in the highly polarized politics of adopting the Constitution.[27]

A more thoughtful novel appeared in 1797 titled *The Algerian Captive*. It was first published anonymously by an American writer

[25] Wilson, Gary. *American Prisoners in the Barbary Nations, 1784-1816.* Pg. 19.

[26] Zeledon, Jason. *The United States and The Barbary Pirates: Adventures in Sexuality, State Building and Nationalism, 1784-1815.* Dissertation, University of California, Santa Barbara, 2016. Retrieved April 11, 2023. https://www.alexandria.ucsb.edu/lib/ark:/48907/f3qj7hcm. Pg. 30.

[27] Zeledon, Jason. *The United States and The Barbary Pirates: Adventures in Sexuality, State Building and Nationalism, 1784-1815.* Pgs. 40-41.

named Royall Tyler. It took the form of a fictional memoir of a doctor who was captured by Barbary pirates from a slave ship off the coast of Africa. The character expresses the sentiment that his own enslavement was perhaps a punishment by God for his participation in the slave trade.[28]

Americans' concern for the plight of prisoners led to fraud. One particularly foul version of it occurred in the 1780s. The fraudster contacted the families of men who were thought to have been lost at sea and claimed to have been in captivity with them. The families were told that their missing loved one was still alive, being held captive by the Barbary pirates, and that a ransom would free them. The perpetrators would offer to help free the man if the family could provide money for the ransom. Some families provided money, only to have the fraudster and their money vanish.[29]

Prisoners experienced harsh conditions and, at times, cruelty. One thing they experienced was shared with their captors: the periodic appearance of bubonic plague. Most of the Barbary cities' population lived in poverty, so their conditions were not a great deal better than the squalor that characterized the prisons where captives were housed. In early 1785, the plague hit Tunis hard, claiming perhaps twenty-five thousand lives. Algiers experienced the plague in 1787, and it killed some of the American captives. Thomas Jefferson, then in France as a diplomat, contacted the Mathurins, one of the Catholic orders dedicated to bringing captives out of Barbary. They were unable to offer any help.[30]

Thomas Jefferson and other American leaders of his time were in a kind of hypocritical bind over slavery. They condemned the Barbary Coast pattern of enslaving white Americans yet owned slaves themselves, even people born in the United States. Over his lifetime, Jefferson owned about six hundred slaves, almost as many as the grand total of American sailors taken prisoner by the Barbary corsairs. This apparent hypocrisy did not seem to have troubled Jefferson much.[31]

---

[28] Zeledon, Jason. *The United States and The Barbary Pirates: Adventures in Sexuality, State Building and Nationalism, 1784-1815.* Pg. 58.

[29] Wilson, Gary. *American Prisoners in the Barbary Nations, 1784-1816.* Pg. 51.

[30] Wilson, Gary. *American Prisoners in the Barbary Nations, 1784-1816.* Pgs. 51-52.

[31] Monsieurs, Roel. *The Causes and Consequences of the First Barbary War 1801-1805.* Pg. 15.

The first American ships bound for Europe and the Mediterranean sailed not long after colonization began. The colonies offered rum, timber, indigo, rice, tobacco, and other products as exports. When the first Americans were captured by Barbary corsairs is not known for certain, but it probably occurred in relatively early colonial times. The corsairs would have made no particular differentiation between English and English colonists.

Colonial shipping was protected from piracy by the Royal Navy. Barbary corsairs did not attack ships flying the British flag because British warships were capable of sinking anything in the Barbary navies.

The British also made treaties with them and sometimes provided money or other items as a kind of annuity. Such payments by Britain were not considered tribute but instead as a kind of retainer. The corsairs could be useful in harassing the commercial shipping of a rival. Britain sometimes warred with the corsairs and sometimes paid tribute. Thus, the status of peace and war with the corsair states quickly changed.

The American colonists lost British protection when they won independence in 1783. During the American Revolution, the Royal Navy and British privateers cleared the Atlantic of most American shipping, and American privateers did substantial damage to British shipping. After the war ended, American shipping quickly recovered. Ships began carrying goods to the Mediterranean, Spain, France, and Italy, and they discovered that the Barbary powers preyed on the smaller and weaker powers. Europe's major maritime powers could easily win a war, but the smaller powers like Sweden, Denmark, the Kingdom of the Two Sicilies, and the United States could not. Preying on the weak was an effective strategy.

Whether the United States should have a standing army and navy was a major issue during the first years after independence. A standing army means a professional force of regular troops and career officers at the ready, and a standing navy means a permanent force of warships, bases, and career officers. Many members of Congress were deeply suspicious of an idea of a standing regular army, thinking a president might be able to use it to seize power and establish tyranny. Such views were based on the presence of British regular troops in the colonies before the American Revolution, seen by many as supporting British tyranny and as something to avoid. The same sentiments existed about a professional navy. There were no major threats to the US at the time, and it was thought that militias could deal with the restive Native Americans in the frontier regions.

The two parties that dominated early American politics were the Federalists and the Republicans. Federalists backed George Washington and John Adams. The Republicans were not the same party as it is today; back then, the party was centered on Thomas Jefferson and his political allies and sometimes were known as the Democratic-Republicans (today's Republican Party was not founded until 1854). The Federalists were opposed to a standing army and navy, and the Jeffersonians reluctantly saw that a navy was a necessity to protect American commerce abroad.

The Federalist view on a standing navy prevailed for several years, but the capture of American ships by Barbary corsairs changed things. Even the Federalists came to the conclusion that a naval force was necessary to respond to the capture of American ships. In 1794, Congress passed the Act to Provide a Naval Armament, which authorized the construction of frigates. The preface to the act specifically mentioned Barbary depredations on American commerce as a way to justify a navy for protection.[32]

The British Royal Navy clearly had the military force to blow the Barbary cities to kingdom come if the British government so desired. However, the British had a number of bases and dependencies in the Mediterranean, some of them taken from the French during the Napoleonic Wars. Those bases needed food supplies, and North Africa was a convenient source of wheat, cattle, and other goods. Their bases included Gibraltar, Minorca, Malta, points in Sicily, and the Ionian Islands. Britain found the Barbary States useful.[33]

American engagements with the corsairs occurred in the context of a global struggle between France and Britain. Both France and Spain were at war with Britain during the American Revolution. The Spanish attacked Gibraltar to no avail, as it was too heavily fortified. Both France and Britain found the continued existence of the Barbary States to be convenient to harass each other's shipping. By then, Spain was a minor

---

[32] Paine, Lincoln. "War is Better Than Tribute." U.S. Naval Institute, *Naval History Magazine* 15 (3), June 2001.Retrieved April 1, 2023. https://www.usni.org/magazines/naval-history-magazine/2001/june/war-better-tribute.

[33] Jamieson, Alan. *Lords of the Sea. A History of the Barbary Corsairs.* Pg. 19.

power. It was a useful ally to France but not a dominant military force.

Another element that considerably affected North Africa was Napoleon's 1798 invasion of Egypt. The French invasion was quite large. It involved thirty-eight thousand troops and an invasion fleet of four hundred ships. Napoleon defeated the Turks in Egypt and Syria, effectively ending Ottoman control of Egypt. Napoleon had taken Malta on the way to Egypt, ending the long existence of the Knights of St. John, and the British took over Malta when Napoleon moved on to Egypt. Malta is only a few hundred miles from both Tripoli and Tunis.

Napoleon sailed back to France in 1799, abandoning his victorious army and leaving it an orphan far from France until its defeat in 1801. The French and British navies fought a huge and bloody naval battle near Egypt, the Battle of the Nile, in 1798 and another off Spain's Atlantic coast at Trafalgar in 1805. The Battle of Trafalgar involved a British fleet under the famed Lord Nelson against a combined Spanish and French fleet. The battle was a decisive British victory, although Nelson was killed. These events left Egypt in a chaotic state, and all of the Maghreb was unsettled.

In 1808, Napoleon forced the Spanish king to abdicate and put his brother on the Spanish throne. The attempt to impose French rule over Spain resulted in the exceedingly bloody Peninsular War (1808–1814). American issues with the Barbary powers occurred in the shadow of these huge events.

During the immense struggle, the Barbary cities prospered due to the nonviolent endeavor of shipping grain to the British bases and dependencies. Peaceful trade probably brought in more money than looting and slaving. Periods of war alternated with periods of peace, and alliances frequently changed.

The threat posed by the Barbary States was important in the early modern United States. In 1784, Congress appointed Thomas Jefferson, John Adams, and Benjamin Franklin as commissioners to try and negotiate what were quaintly referred to as "treaties of amity and commerce" with the nations of Europe and the Mediterranean. They were also charged with making agreements with the Barbary States.[34]

---

[34] Huff, Elizabeth. "First Barbary War." August, 2011. *Thomas Jefferson Encyclopedia.* Retrieved April 13, 2023. https://www.monticello.org/research-education/thomas-jefferson-encyclopedia/first-barbary-war/.

The three commissioners were already in Europe, and one of them had a vast amount of diplomatic experience. Franklin spent more than twenty years in Britain and France during his long life. John Adams was in Britain, France, and the Netherlands from 1778 to 1788, and Jefferson was in Europe from 1784 to 1789. This might be the only time that two future US presidents served together on a diplomatic team. The options available were few, with a penny-pinching Congress back home and no navy abroad. The only logical way to prevent Barbary corsairs from preying on American ships was the centuries-old practice of tribute. In 1784, Jefferson opined that he doubted Americans would be willing to pay tribute and that he thought that war was better than tribute.[35]

Adams, Franklin, and John Jay had signed the Treaty of Paris in 1783, which officially ended the American Revolutionary War. The various American representatives in Europe tried to retain British protection for American shipping, but Britain refused. The commissioners approached France, Spain, and the Netherlands about protecting American merchant ships, but none of them were interested in helping protect a fast-growing competitor.[36]

The commissioners did have some success with the Barbary Coast. They signed a treaty with Morocco that involved a surprisingly small tribute payment. The treaty made the Atlantic regions near Morocco safer for American merchant ships, and American ships could call at Moroccan ports. Morocco's Tangier was a convenient port, as it was right at the entrance to the Straits of Gibraltar. Tangier had once been Portuguese and then English, but Morocco controlled it by this time.

Two American schooners with a total of twenty-three crewmen were taken by Barbary corsairs in 1784. By 1793, 11 more American ships had been taken by the corsairs, adding 119 more captives to those already at Algiers. That was a tiny portion of the large numbers of American sailors at sea, but their situation aroused great sympathy. American diplomats negotiated with the dey of Algiers, concluding an agreement in 1795 that included $642,500 in cash and an annual supply of naval stores payment for releasing American captives. North Africa

[35] Huff, Elizabeth. "First Barbary War."

[36] Kitzen, Michael. "Money Bags and Cannon Balls: The Origin of the Tripolitan War, 1795-1801." Journal of the Early Republic 16 (4), Winter 1996. 601-24. JSTOR access, April 11, 2023. Pg. 603.

had to import most of its naval stores, which included wood, tar, and ropes, so the tribute in naval supplies was significant and helped keep the corsairs ready to sail. The dey also agreed to assist Americans in negotiating with Tunis and Tripoli.

The original American treaty with Tunis had some peculiar conditions. One was that Tripolitan ships visiting the United States would pay a 3 percent tax and that American ships visiting Tunis would pay the same. There were no known ships from Tripoli docking in the US. The bey wanted $107,000 in naval supplies, weapons, money, and jewels. Every time the bey saluted an American ship, he was to receive one barrel of gunpowder for each cannon used in the salute. He also had the right to take any American ship in his harbor into his service to deliver dispatches or cargo to any Mediterranean port. The jewels to pay the bey were purchased in London, and whether the gunpowder bonus for salutes actually occurred seems to be unknown.[37]

Prisoners did what they could to get themselves released or at least their condition bettered. In Algiers, in one batch of thirteen American captives, eleven petitioned King George III, asking to be redeemed because they were not really American. They claimed to have been born British and to have fought for the British in the American Revolution, which might have been true. The petition was probably handed to the British consul in Algiers, but nothing came of it.[38]

Ransoming prisoners was expensive. In 1790, it cost the United States $59,496 to ransom a group of prisoners consisting of three captains, two mates, three passengers, and fourteen sailors. It's difficult to interpret those amounts in current money, but using a contemporary inflation calculator, that $59,496 would be roughly about $2,000,000 today, or about $90,000 apiece. To compare the ransom figures with other expenses in the 1790s, it cost about $600,000 to build a 44-gun frigate.[39]

---

[37] Vivian, Cassandra. "William Eaton: To the Shores of Tripoli." Academia.edu. Retrieved April 20, 2023. https://www.academia.edu/17964588/William_Eaton_To_the_Shores_of_Tripoli. Pg. 64.

[38] Zeledon, Jason. The United States and The Barbary Pirates: Adventures in Sexuality, State Building and Nationalism, 1784-1815. Pg. 48.

[39] Lazerowitz, Evan. "America's Second War of Independence: The Barbary Pirate Wars and their Effect on American Geopolitical Power." Georgetown University Law Center, Washington, D.C. December 4, 2008. 1-15. Retrieved April, 2023. https://papers.ssrn.com/sol3/papers.cfm?abstract_id=1955322. Pgs. 7 & 16.

The tribute money was slow to arrive, mostly because Congress was slow to make the needed appropriations, and in 1786, Algiers threatened war. American consuls promised Algiers the tribute would arrive soon and promised to have a 36-gun frigate built for the dey and deliver it to Algiers. These promises soothed the dey, and the prospect of war receded. However, the Tripolitans were angered at not getting as good a deal.[40]

Tripoli was believed to be the weakest of the three Barbary States, but its naval strength increased with the addition of two 18-gun corvettes and a large supply of gunpowder and other naval supplies. These were delivered to Tripoli as part of tribute agreements between Denmark and Norway. The pasha ruling in Tripoli was doing his best to make his city more powerful.[41]

In 1797, the US appointed new consuls to the Barbary cities. William Eaton was appointed consul to Tunis, James Cathcart to Tripoli, and Joel Barlow to Algiers. Consuls were not formal ambassadors, although they were part of the State Department. They were agents of the Consular Service, which existed until the 1890s. Their purpose was to assist American sailors and promote trade. During times of war, a consul or citizen of another country might agree to perform consular duties. The consuls did their best to help American prisoners with clothes and sometimes money and pressured the US government for ransom money. There were consuls in many port cities all over the globe, including places far from any US Embassy. Consuls were not always American citizens.

One appointment made to represent the US in Algiers was filled by John Paul Jones, the naval hero of the American Revolution. He was living in Paris after having spent several tumultuous years in the Russian Navy. George Washington appointed him to be a commissioner to the Barbary States. Jones knew French, which had been the language of the court in Russia and was also commonly spoken by consuls and merchants in Algiers. However, Jones died before he had the chance to

---

[40] Kitzen, Michael. "Money Bags and Cannon Balls: The Origin of the Tripolitan War, 1795-1801." Pgs. 604-605.

[41] Kitzen, Michael. "Money Bags and Cannon Balls: The Origin of the Tripolitan War, 1795-1801." Pg. 609.

travel to Algiers.[42]

In the Barbary States, the US consuls negotiated with local rulers, helped captives as best they could, and frequently corresponded with officials in Washington, reporting on everything from politics and the weather to the state of relations among the Barbary States. Several of the American consuls were once prisoners and might have learned Arabic. The languages spoken in the corsair cities included dialects of Arabic, Turkish, French, Italian, and Spanish.

One of the American consuls had a highly unusual history. James Cathcart was captured when the US ship *Maria* was captured by an Algerian corsair in 1785. He was seventeen and was enslaved. Cathcart somehow impressed his Muslim captors. He became a palace gardener and then a coffee brewer to an influential Algerian before finally becoming the chief secretary to the dey (the ruler of Algiers). He learned Arabic well, but that was not the most unusual thing about his captivity. He was allowed to set up some businesses, probably coffee shops, and he made money. Cathcart made enough money to buy a ship and sail back to the United States. He was probably the only American ever to do so.[43]

In October of 1793, the dey of Algiers grew tired of waiting for the promised tribute from the Americans. He sent out a flotilla, consisting of a brig and three xebecs, to go after American ships in the Atlantic. The xebecs were three-masted lateen-rigged ships, roughly the equivalent of a schooner and capable of carrying about twenty guns and a sizable crew. They captured eleven American ships, including four on a single day, and about a hundred crewmen were captured.[44]

The Algerian captors were not simply brutal slave owners. They were highly attuned to the possibilities of ransom. A slave working in the harbor had a certain value, but the folks back home might want him so much they'd pay high ransoms (all of the known American captives in

[42] Daly, Robert. The Diplomatic Relations of the United States with the Barbary Coast, 1790-1801. Pg. 38.

[43] Boot, Max. *Savage Wars of Peace. Small Wars and the Rise of American Power.* New York: Basic Books, 2002. Pg. 9.

[44] Prom, William. "The Seventh Frigate." *Naval History Magazine* 34 (4), April 17, 2020. Retrieved April 17, 2023. https://www.usni.org/magazines/naval-history-magazine/2020/august/seventh-frigate.

Barbary were male). One of the American captives in Algiers was Richard O'Brien, skipper of one of the captured ships. O'Brien repeatedly wrote letters to Thomas Jefferson, who was then secretary of state. The letters were given to the American consul and sent to Washington. O'Brien's accounts of captivity prompted Congress to consider paying tribute. After being ransomed, O'Brien was later appointed a US consul.[45]

The American public was widely sympathetic to the prisoners' situation, and letters like those from O'Brien highlighted their plight. In many communities, from Savannah to Baltimore to Boston, people came together to raise money. One way was for a theater to donate the proceeds from a night's performance. A Boston theater did that and raised $887.25, which was deposited in a bank. A letter was then sent to George Washington saying the money was available.[46]

The brief state of war with Algiers had an impact on Congress. In March 1794, Congress passed the Naval Armament Act, authorizing six frigates to be built for the purpose of defending American commerce. The frigates were to be named *Constitution, United States, President, Constellation, Chesapeake,* and *Congress.* The names of these ships reverberate through the US Navy's history. Work on the frigates was suspended when news of the treaty arrived, but later authorizations allowed three frigates to be finished.

Despite Cathcart's rather positive experience, being a captive often meant being a slave, and slaves often experienced hard labor, poor food, living quarters full of rats and lice, capricious and brutal discipline, and sometimes sexual exploitation. In 1796, the dey released his American prisoners after a treaty was agreed upon. Of the 119 original captives, 88 survived to be released, the rest having died of disease. Diseases easily spread in almost all cities in the Mediterranean, and epidemics were common.[47]

Of the 31 of those 119 who died before release, most were probably victims of the bubonic plague. As far as it is known, none were killed by their captors, although the poor food and appalling living conditions

[45] Daly, Robert. The Diplomatic Relations of the United States with the Barbary Coast, 1790-1801. Pg. 35.

[46] Wilson, Gary. *American Prisoners in the Barbary Nations, 1784-1816.* Pg. 79.

[47] Boot, Max. *Savage Wars of Peace. Small Wars and the Rise of American Power.* Pg. 11.

doubtlessly contributed to the deaths by disease.

Freedom was not easy at first. A number of the men immediately joined the crews of merchant ships. The remainder were sent to Marseilles, and the French required an eighty-day quarantine before allowing them in France, a precaution that was wise. The ship taking them to France sailed back to Algiers shortly after leaving because one of the passengers showed symptoms of the plague. The passenger was left at Algiers and died. While in quarantine, the American consul arranged for them to obtain clothes and provided an allowance of thirty-five cents a day.[48]

In November, sixty-five of the prisoners left France on a ship bound for Philadelphia. The voyage took months, and when they arrived, ice in the Delaware River prevented them from landing. Once they landed, they were enthusiastically welcomed home.

Returning captives must have been glad to reach home shores, but their personal situation was often difficult. Their families might have moved or died, and their spouses might have remarried. Some had been captive for more than a decade and had heard nothing of home. Many were destitute upon arrival, and publishing autobiographical accounts was one way of becoming solvent again. Charities helped, but there were no helpful grants from the skinflint Congress.

The treaty with Algiers was negotiated by American consul Jacob Sheaf. It specified a $600,000 ransom for the American prisoners and $21,000 in annual tribute. After some months had passed, the tribute was late, and Algiers was upset and threatened war. Algiers had a considerable income from such payments. The Dutch, Danes, and Swedes were paying $24,000 a year each. France paid $133,000, Britain $280,000, and Spain $3,000,000.[49]

The American consul met with the dey's representatives and worked out an agreement for an extension to the tribute. The consul offered to provide Algiers with a 24-gun ship, and the dey countered with a 36-gun ship, which was agreed to. The dey also agreed to help with negotiations with both Tunis and Tripoli.

[48] Wilson, Gary. *American Prisoners in the Barbary Nations, 1784-1816.* Pg. 114.

[49] Prom, William. "The Seventh Frigate."

The 36-gun frigate promised to Algiers in the treaty has a story worth recounting because it includes most of the issues related to the Barbary Wars in miniature. The frigate, named the *Crescent* by its builders, was built in Portsmouth, New Hampshire, and was essentially the seventh frigate added to the authorized six. Contracts for building the ships were distributed among several states to spread out the business, which is still the way the US Navy does things. This was almost certainly the only time an American shipyard built a ship that was intended to become a Muslim corsair's ship.

The *Crescent* was built to the same quality standards as the others but apparently was built to be as small as possible and yet be rated a 36-gun ship. It displaced 600 tons compared to the 1,600 tons of the 44-gun frigates. She was armed with twenty-four 9-pounder guns and twelve other cannons. This was probably as formidable an armament as any ship in the Algerian fleet but rather light for an American frigate.

The ship was completed and ready for its voyage to North Africa in January 1798. A crew and officers were assigned to sail it to Algiers. It reached Gibraltar in mid-February and arrived in Algiers on February 26th, with a formal presentation made on March 1st, 1798. The *Crescent* carried varied cargo to Algiers, including $100,000 worth of gunpowder and other naval supplies and 30,000 pounds of cannonballs. It also carried $180,000 in silver dollars, which equates to 4.5 tons of silver dollars packed tight in 26 barrels. When the frigate arrived in Algiers, there were three American merchant ships in the harbor taking temporary refuge from Spanish and French privateers. The irony must have been evident: American ships taking refuge in a Barbary harbor to escape the attention of European pirates.[50]

The adventure was not quite over. The officers and crew that sailed the *Crescent* to Algiers sailed home on an American merchant ship, the *Sarah*. On the way, they were fired on by a French privateer and barely escaped.

The *Crescent* had an unremarkable record in Algerian service. She went on several cruises and, as far as it is known, participated in no captures and no battles. The ship was poorly maintained and soon became unusable. The *Crescent* was broken up in 1806.[51]

---

[50] Prom, William. "The Seventh Frigate."

[51] Prom, William. "The Seventh Frigate."

One odd factor in the 1780s and early 1790s was that Portugal protected American shipping in the region. Portugal had not signed a peace treaty with Algiers, although Spain had done so. The Portuguese fleet patrolled off Portugal and in the Straits of Gibraltar. The US Congress sent a letter to Queen Maria I expressing its gratitude. When the Portuguese signed an agreement with the Barbary States in 1793, that protection was lost.[52]

A tactic that seems to have often worked was American ships flying the flag of another nation, usually Britain. They also sometimes forged British passes. The corsairs could not tell the British from the Americans because they both spoke the same language.

Glitches in the tribute system caused problems; a delay caused by circumstances could be interpreted by a dey as reluctance to pay. One problem was paying in specie—actual coins—because there was barely enough to grease commerce, let alone enough to allow large amounts of coins to be accumulated. Sometimes, there simply weren't enough coins. There were other problems too. In 1796, the American ship *Sophia* was on its way from Lisbon, Portugal, to Algiers carrying $200,000 in gold coins to pay due and overdue American tributes to the dey. It was captured by a corsair from Tripoli and taken there. Its crew was imprisoned, as was the passenger, the American consul. Yusuf Pasha decided to release the ship, its crew, and the $200,000 rather than risk war with Algiers.[53]

The US Navy was, in effect, re-founded in the 1790s. Despite official claims that it dates back to 1775, there were no ships in service and no officers or crews. Officers were appointed in 1794 with the new frigates Congress finally decided to fund. The officers were veterans of the American Revolutionary War, so none of them were new to war.

The first naval war of the independent United States was actually not with the Barbary States. It was with revolutionary France and was called the Quasi-War, lasting from 1798 to 1800. The combat was all at sea and took place almost entirely in the Caribbean and off the eastern US coast. The conflict got its unique name because it wasn't quite a full war, and there was no declaration of war by either side. The French

---

[52] Ribiero, Jorge Martins. "Conflict and Peace in the Mediterranean: Barbary Privateering in the Late 18th and Early 19th Centuries." Pgs. 164-166.

[53] Wilson, Gary. *American Prisoners in the Barbary Nations, 1784-1816.* Pg. 115.

revolutionary government was at war with Britain and issued permits for privateers who were swarming in the Caribbean seeking British shipping. However, they were not opposed to capturing American ships as well. The French owned several islands in the Caribbean, such as Haiti, and thus had convenient local bases. The US did not yet own New Orleans or Florida, so the nearest convenient harbor for US Navy warships was probably Charleston, South Carolina,

The friendly France that had allied with Americans during their revolution had fractured, as France had become revolutionary itself, executing the king and tens of thousands of others. France and Britain went to war yet again in 1792, and the US tried to remain neutral, but the rising number of privateers so close to the country provoked anger. That was one of the reasons why the miserly Congress loosened the purse strings a little and built the famed six frigates; the other was the Barbary threat.[54]

There was little conflict with actual French warships. In November 1798, the USS *Retaliation* surrendered to two French frigates without a shot being fired. The American ship apparently thought the French ships were British and came so close that there would have been no chance of survival. The captain was William Bainbridge, an able officer who had perhaps the worst luck in American naval history, with later highly unfortunate incidents occurring while commanding the frigates *George Washington* and *Philadelphia*.

The most notable battle of the Quasi-War was when the frigate USS *Constellation* met with the French frigate *L'Insurgente*. The French ship had been heavily damaged in a storm and surrendered after a couple of broadsides from the American warship. It was taken to Saint Kitts as a prize of war.

The US Navy made a dent in the number of French privateers, capturing at least eighty-six of them in 1799 and 1800. About three hundred American merchant ships were taken by French privateers.

One other notable battle involved the sloop USS *Delaware*. It captured the large French privateer vessel *La Croyable* off the New Jersey coast in 1798. Its captain was Stephen Decatur Sr., father of Stephen Decatur Jr., the most successful American officer of the Barbary

---

[54] U.S.S. Constitution Museum. "The Quasi-War with France (1798-1801)." https://ussconstitutionmuseum.org/major-events/the-quasi-war-with-france/.

Wars.

This little-known war ended in 1800 with the Treaty of Mortefontaine, although it was not ratified by US Congress until the following year. The cruises against the French privateers provided a training ground before the US Navy embarked on the faraway Mediterranean missions.[55]

The damage inflicted by the French privateers was actually considerably greater than anything inflicted by the Barbary corsairs. The rather disproportionate attention paid to the Barbary situation probably reflects the popular interest in captivity narratives about white Christian sailors captured and enslaved by African Muslims and the nation's embarrassment at paying protection money.

Tribute due to the Barbary States was usually carried by a warship, which was safer and prevented an attack while the ship was in transit. In 1800, the USS frigate *George Washington* sailed to Algiers, carrying overdue tribute. The captain was William Bainbridge (1774–1833), a young officer with a good record, although, as we mentioned, the ship he commanded in the Quasi-War was surrendered to the French. He was another American officer who had personal experience of being a prisoner, as he was captured in the Quasi-War. The *George Washington* had been built as a merchant ship but was bought by the US Navy in 1798 and converted into a frigate. When the ship reached Algiers, Bainbridge made the crucial mistake of letting the local pilot guide the ship to anchor under the fortress guns, which made the frigate highly vulnerable.

The dey was not happy with the slowness of the American tribute and threatened Bainbridge. After the frigate spent some time in the harbor, the dey summoned Bainbridge and told him his frigate was going to sail to Istanbul with a cargo of people and presents for the sultan, a cruise of about 1,700 nautical miles (a nautical mile is 1.15 statute miles, the kind used on land). Bainbridge could not refuse since the *George Washington* was anchored within close range of a fortress bristling with heavy guns. He reluctantly agreed to the demand.

The resulting cargo was probably the most bizarre ever carried by an American warship. The nature of the Algerian transported is described slightly differently by different historians; the chief among the passengers

---

[55] U.S.S. Constitution Museum. "The Quasi-War with France (1798-1801)."

might have been an ambassador to the Porte (the Ottoman diplomatic service), or he might have been a wealthy hostage. There were about sixty Algerians, apparently many of them servants of the ambassador, and there were one hundred African slaves. There were also about sixty women, some or all of them in a harem. Then there were the animals. They included one hundred sheep, four horses, four lions, four tigers, four antelopes, and twelve parrots. The sheep were probably provisions for the Muslim passengers because the usual US Navy fare of pickled pork would have been rejected. The "tigers" are puzzling since they are not native to Africa; they might have been leopards or cheetahs. The cargo included an unknown but very large amount of gold, jewels, and money. The listing of these unusual things was made by the US consul in Algiers.[56]

Aside from the bizarre aspects of the cargo, it was also exceedingly valuable. The dey probably thought that the frigate offered an opportunity to send valued people and other valuables in a secure way. It also might have meant that he trusted the Americans in an odd way, or perhaps he threatened harm to captives if his wish was not complied with. A pirate would have dumped the people and animals overboard once at sea and sailed off with the valuables.

So, the *George Washington* became a combination of warship, slave ship, treasure ship, harem ship, and floating zoo. With two hundred crewmen, more than two hundred passengers, and one hundred or so animals, the ship must have been noisy and probably stank after the first couple of days. The Algerians insisted that the frigate face the proper direction to Mecca for daily prayers, and the voyage began with the American flag being hauled down and the Algerian banner being raised.

Once at sea and out of the range of the Algiers fortress artillery, Bainbridge raised the American flag. The frigate arrived in Istanbul with no problems on the way. The American flag was apparently unknown in the Ottoman city. The *George Washington* was the first American warship to anchor in the Golden Horn.

The frigate sailed back to Algiers with dispatches from the sultan to the dey, but Bainbridge was careful to stay out of range of the port's artillery this time. However, his adventure was not quite over. Algiers was

[56] Zeledon, Jason. *The United States and The Barbary Pirates: Adventures in Sexuality, State Building and Nationalism, 1784-1815.* Pgs. 81-82.

considering war with France and threatened to imprison the French citizens in Algiers. The dey relented, and fifty-six French citizens boarded the American frigate, which then sailed to a Spanish port and let them ashore there. Reportedly, Napoleon Bonaparte was grateful[57]

When the ship sailed into an American port later in the year, and its story became known, there was national embarrassment and anger. Bainbridge is reported to have said he never wanted to visit Algiers again unless the tribute he was delivering was cannonballs. However, the zoo cruise was not the last time Bainbridge would be humiliated on the African coast. Part of the people's outrage might have stemmed from the fact the frigate was named after the hero of the American Revolution and the first president. Shortly after, the frigate was decommissioned and sold, so it did not participate in the Barbary Wars. Why it was sold is not known.

In October 1800, corsairs from Tripoli captured an American merchant ship, the brig *Catharine*. The pasha released the ship and its crew as a gesture of goodwill and also a warning. Yusuf Pasha made it plain to the American consul that he was unhappy at getting less tribute money than Algiers or Tunis and that if the situation was not corrected, war would ensue.

---

[57] Wilson, Gary. *American Prisoners in the Barbary Nations, 1784-1816.* Pg. 141.

Chapter 3 – War with Tripoli
(1801–1803)

In 1801, President Thomas Jefferson ordered the US Navy to send a squadron of warships to the Mediterranean to deal with the Barbary problem. Sending a sizable naval force four thousand miles was a major effort in administration and supply, but Jefferson and others thought it worthwhile even though it was not known if a war had officially broken out. Congress was not in session, so it could not authorize the mission, but Jefferson justified his actions as being needed. This set a precedent that a president could order the US Navy into action. Congress soon after gave its approval.[58]

In a way, the huge effort made by the United States in the Barbary Wars was not needed. The depredations of the Barbary corsairs on American shipping were minor when compared to the damage inflicted by British and French privateers. From 1785 to 1815, the Barbary corsairs captured thirty-five American ships and took about seven hundred officers and crew prisoners. Between 1793 and 1812, the Royal Navy stopped many American ships, looking for deserters. The process of taking a man and forcing him into the crew of another ship is called "impressment." During that span, the British impressed about six thousand sailors from American ships, including three from a US Navy

---

[58] Monsieurs, Roel. *The Causes and Consequences of the First Barbary War 1801-1805.* Pg. 64.

gunboat en route to the Mediterranean in 1805.[59]

Yusuf Karamanli Pasha of Tripoli was an ambitious leader. Tripoli was the weakest of the three Barbary powers, and he was determined to strengthen it. He hired Spanish shipwrights to build new ships, and he worked to increase the old trans-Saharan trade in ivory, gold, and slaves, with Tripoli as its Mediterranean terminus.

He was angry at the slow arrival of American tribute. In February 1799, James Cathcart arrived as the new American consul. He negotiated with Yusuf and agreed to pay $10,000 in lieu of the promised naval stores, $8,000 more in lieu of a promised ship, and an additional $5,500 for gifts to the pasha.[60]

Peace ensued for a time, but an unhappy Yusuf met again with Consul Cathcart, who had the advantage of being fluent in Arabic. Cathcart knew a war was coming, so he sent warning letters to the American consuls in Tunis and Algiers, as well as to the consuls in Spain, France, the Italian states, and elsewhere. He notified the British of impending hostilities, made arrangements with the Danish consul in Tripoli for clothing and allowances for American prisoners, and then left.[61]

Yusuf declared war on the United States on May 14th, 1801. The declaration was made by sending men to chop down the flagpole at the house of the American consul. Yusuf claimed that Tripoli had observed every condition of the previous agreements, including releasing the *Catherine* and its crew. The promised tribute had not arrived, and Yusuf wanted more, so he declared war.[62]

Before we dive into the conflicts of the First Barbary War, let's take a moment to discuss the weapons and ships the Americans had on hand. As mentioned, in the 1790s, Congress was split between spending as little money as possible and creating enough of a naval force to offer some protection to American ships. Congress decided to build six frigates, three 44s and three 36s, which refer to the number of cannons the ship carried (the broadside weaponry). Ships also carried a few other

---

[59] Paine, Lincoln. "War is Better Than Tribute."

[60] Paine, Lincoln. "War is Better Than Tribute."

[61] Wilson, Gary. *American Prisoners in the Barbary Nations, 1784-1816.* Pg. 154.

[62] Zeledon, Jason. *The United States and The Barbary Pirates: Adventures in Sexuality, State Building and Nationalism, 1784-1815.* Pgs. 91-92.

kinds of artillery, so the 44s had more than fifty guns. The naval artillery on the American frigates was a combination of 24-pounder long guns and 32-pounder carronades, which were more effective in close combat. The use of pound with the cannons refers to the official weight of the cannonballs the guns fired.

These weapons were much more complicated than placing a cannonball and powder charge down the barrel of a carronade and firing it. There were various kinds of shot depending on whether the purpose was to damage rigging, puncture the hull, clear a deck of enemy personnel, or bombard a fortification. For example, a typical round iron cannonball could puncture the hull of an enemy ship. Two cannonballs welded to a bar, looking something like a weightlifter's barbell, were used to shred sails and rigging—if done well, it damaged an enemy ship's ability to maneuver. A sort of a can full of smaller iron or lead balls, called grapeshot because it looked like a bunch of grapes, was an anti-personnel round and could be fired to clear an enemy ship's deck of crewmen. Warships also stationed sharpshooters in crow's nests up on the masts, and boarding parties used cutlasses and pistols.

Some artillery was specialist. The bomb ketches (bomb ships) the US Navy borrowed from Sicily had one very large mortar fixed on the ship that fired a large shot in a high arc, like a modern howitzer. The mortar ammunition included rounds designed to explode when they landed, causing blast damage and shrapnel. These were for bombardment rather than battering down fortification walls. Both long guns and mortars could fire hot shots, cannonballs heated over a grill-like apparatus to a red heat that had an incendiary effect if they hit the right target and might blow up an enemy ship if they hit a powder magazine. These were dangerous to use, but if loaded correctly, the danger was minimal. Gun crews were experts at using these weapons.

The gun crews on American warships were often well drilled and often performed better than crews on enemy warships. They could fire their cannons more rapidly and with better accuracy. US Navy ships and crews in the Barbary Wars were better trained, had better equipment, and had much better ships than the Barbary corsairs. The corsairs performed uniformly badly against American warships. Artillery in the massive forts protecting the Barbary cities was a different matter and was considerably more dangerous. All the Barbary States had experienced bombardment by enemy fleets and had stout fortifications to resist them.

The few American frigates were formidable. The biggest were the 44-gun sister ships of the USS *Constitution*. This frigate was rated at 44-guns but carried more than that. The ship was armed with twenty-four 32-pounder carronades and thirty 24-pound long guns arranged on two gun decks. The carronades had a much shorter range, as they were accurate only up to about four hundred yards, but were devastating in close combat. The long guns were for broadsides at a considerably greater distance. The frigate also carried a long gun called a "bow chaser" that fired ahead rather than from the sides, and it was used in pursuits. That's fifty-five formidable guns on a 44-gun ship, and that's the main reason American frigates did rather well in ship-to-ship duels with the French and British.

The *Constitution*'s dimensions give an idea of the size of these ships. She was 207 feet long, had a beam of 43 feet, and had a draft of 24 feet, which means the water had to be more than 24 feet deep for the frigate to sail safely. It was 172 feet from the deck to the top of the mainmast, which means lookouts up high could see a great distance. In bad weather, sailors would be the equivalent of seventeen stories high as they handled topsails on masts wildly weaving from side to side. The *Constitution* displaced 1,900 tons and 2,200 tons when loaded. It had a crew of around four hundred officers and men.[63]

These frigates became famous and were involved in the Quasi-War with France, the Barbary Wars, and the War of 1812. The most famous is the USS *Constitution,* which later became known as Old Ironsides due to British cannonballs seemingly bouncing off the thick oak planking on the frigate's sides. The frigates were built by a genius shipbuilder named Joshua Humphreys and an equally talented marine architect named Josiah Fox. American shipyards traditionally produced quality ships. The frigates were significantly faster and more powerful than similar ships in the British and other navies. Americans did not build enough warships, but the ones they built were exceptionally good.[64]

Sailing ships had one major advantage over their coal- and oil-powered successors. The only fuel they needed was the wind, and they could stay at sea for months and maintain a blockade for an extended period as long as they had loaded sufficient stores of food and water.

---

[63] U.S.S. Constitution Museum. "The Quasi-War with France (1798-1801)."

[64] Boot, Max. *Savage Wars of Peace. Small Wars and the Rise of American Power.* Pg. 10.

After some weeks at sea, the water often became foul, and the usual rations of pickled pork and hard biscuits were often infested with weevils. The ships also almost always had vermin, like rats and lice, although the ship's cat helped keep the rats under control. The condition called scurvy, a serious lack of vitamin C, could result from long periods at sea with a poor diet, and it often did more harm to a ship's crew than enemy action.

Service in the American Navy was somewhat less arduous than in the Royal Navy, where discipline was severe. Officers sometimes held seamen in contempt, and food and living conditions were sometimes very bad. American service paid somewhat better, and there appears to have been less of a class difference between officers and crew, perhaps because so many American officers had the same common roots in the New England sailing tradition as the seamen did. A portion of many American crews originated as deserters from British ships who preferred the better conditions on the American ships.

Although US Navy discipline was rarely as harsh as in the Royal Navy, it could still be severe. The whip was used as punishment well into the 1800s, and a captain held the literal power of life and death over his crew. In the case of mutiny or other serious crimes, a captain and his officers could hold a court-martial, condemn a sailor to death, and hang him from a yardarm. However, that was extremely rare aboard US ships.

The issue of British seamen deserting Royal Navy warships to join an American ship was a serious one for the British, who had a shortage of crews during their wars with France. This was the major reason British warships sometimes halted American merchant ships at sea and examined the crew's documents. Sailors the British officers thought were British were forced off the ships and taken aboard theirs. Far more men were removed from American ships than were ever taken prisoner by the Barbary corsairs, and this high-handed policy by the Royal Navy was the major cause of the War of 1812.

But back to the topic at hand. The first American force sent to the Barbary Coast was commanded by Commodore Richard Dale (1756–1826), who had served in the American Revolution with the famed John Paul Jones on the *Bonhomme Richard*. Dale had gone to sea at age twelve and served with the Continental Navy in the American Revolution. He knew something about being held prisoner, having been captured by the British and taken to Britain as a prisoner of war. After a year, he escaped, was recaptured, escaped again, and fled to France, where he joined John Paul Jones. Dale's overall achievements in the Barbary Wars were rather modest, considering his record of distinguished service.

In July 1801, Dale's force sailed for the Barbary Coast. The squadron left the US on June 2nd and arrived at Gibraltar on July 1st; it was a four-week voyage, which was typical for the time. War had not yet been declared, at least as far as the Americans knew. Dale's squadron consisted of three frigates and three smaller ships, which was not very powerful by European standards but enough to match Tripoli's corsairs.

Because of the long voyage times, there was a delay in information being exchanged between North Africa and the United States. Even the fastest ships took weeks to sail that distance. Dale's instructions took into account that by the time he arrived, the situation might have changed. Dale's force had several missions. One of them was to deliver some of the long-overdue tribute to Algiers and Tunis. He was to assure the dey of Algiers that the balance of the overdue tribute would soon arrive.

He was also to sail to Tripoli, deliver a letter to the pasha, and take some money to Consul Cathcart to make a "gift" to the pasha. That is if the US and Tripoli were still at peace. Commanders and consuls had considerable leeway because communication was slow. A four-week crossing of the Atlantic one way meant that sending letters back to Washington and getting a response and new orders took at least two months—and the ship carrying the communication did not always make it.

Dale's instructions included the possibility that war might have been declared by Tripoli. If he found that to be the case, he was instructed to "chastise their insolence ... by sinking, burning or destroying their ships and vessels wherever you shall find them."[65]

Upon arriving in Gibraltar, the American force found that Tripoli had indeed declared war on the United States. Dale found two Tripolitan corsairs in Gibraltar and blockaded them. He also briefly and unsuccessfully blockaded Tripoli itself. One of the ships was the *Mashouda*, a formidable Tripolitan vessel. It was commanded by Murad Rais, who had once been known as Peter Lyle, a Scottish sailor who deserted a Royal Navy ship. Lyle converted to Islam and served as the

---

[65] Huff, Elizabeth. "First Barbary War."

admiral of the Tripolitan fleet.[66]

The *Mashouda* was a solid ship. It had been built in Sweden, captured by corsairs, and then refitted as a frigate. It was blockaded in Gibraltar for two years. The British would not sell them provisions, so the crew was on short rations or starving. About 150 of the crew mutinied; the mutineers were rounded up by the British and sent to Morocco.[67]

The force under Dale was fairly powerful but did not accomplish much. The most notable naval action of the squadron was on August 1st, 1802, when a ship-to-ship duel occurred between the USS *Enterprise* and the *Tripoli.*

The *Enterprise* was a 12-gun schooner of about 135 tons displacement and with a crew of 90, which was evenly matched by the Barbary corsair ship. One difference was that the corsair ship was lateen-rigged and was a type of ship called a polacca. The Tripolitan ship was cruising for prey, and the American schooner was on a mission to Malta. Apparently, the US Navy ship was flying the Royal Navy flag and was able to close on the corsair ship. At the time, flying the flag of another nation was a permissible and common ruse, and the national flag would be unfurled once the warship came in close. It worked because, at a distance, the nationality of a sailing ship was not easy to determine except by a large flag.

The preferred corsair style of combat was to close with the enemy and board in an attack with pistols, sabers, and cutlasses. The American style was to fire broadsides from a short distance to batter the enemy into submission.

The combat lasted three hours and resulted in half the Muslim crew becoming casualties. Thirty of them were killed. No Americans were injured. The American commander, Lieutenant Andrew Sterrett, had orders to intercept Tripoli corsairs but was not authorized to take any prisoners. His crew boarded the *Tripoli,* cut down the masts, threw its armament overboard, and allowed it just enough equipment to sail slowly back to Tripoli.[68]

---

[66] Paine, Lincoln. "War is Better Than Tribute."

[67] Wilson, Gary. *American Prisoners in the Barbary Nations, 1784-1816.* Pg. 158.

[68] Boot, Max. *Savage Wars of Peace. Small Wars and the Rise of American Power.* Pg. 14.

The pasha was not pleased with his ship's performance. Defeat was not acceptable. He had the polacca's captain ride through the city streets backward on a donkey with the guts of a sheep hung from his neck. The captain was derided by the people as he was led through the streets. At the end of his parade of shame, he was given five hundred strokes on the soles of his feet. This punishment was known as a bastinado.[69]

The *Enterprise* engaged another Tripolitan ship in June 1803. The engagement lasted forty-five minutes but had a much different result. A lucky shot hit the Tripolitan's magazine or some container of gunpowder because the corsair ship blew up.[70]

Commodore Dale had already sailed home by this point. In 1802, he left behind the *Essex* and the *Philadelphia*. He was replaced by another strong naval force commanded by Commodore Richard Morris, which sailed from Hampton Roads in April of 1802. Morris (1768–1815) had commanded a ship in the Quasi-War with France, but his career was not very distinguished. He came from a well-connected New York family, and his father was one of the signers of the Declaration of Independence. Morris had six powerful ships, but like Dale, he did not have more than the opportunity to engage the enemy on a regular basis. However, Morris appears to have been uninterested in campaigning.

Morris brought along his wife, maid, and family, and on reaching Europe, he settled his family in Gibraltar, where he apparently enjoyed the hospitality of the British and officers of the Royal Navy stationed there. His period of command was notable only for its inaction and incompetence. He seems to have spent considerably more time ashore than on board his ship. The American consul in Tunis cynically complained of Morris's force, saying, "What have they done but dance and wench?"[71]

While Morris was remarkably ineffective as commander of the Mediterranean squadron, there were some contributing factors. One was that President Jefferson did not send the strongest force possible with

[69] Boot, Max. *Savage Wars of Peace. Small Wars and the Rise of American Power.* Pg. 14.

[70] Zeledon, Jason. *The United States and The Barbary Pirates: Adventures in Sexuality, State Building and Nationalism, 1784-1815.* Pg. 125.

[71] Fowler, Jr., William. "The Navy's Barbary War Crucible." U.S. Naval Institute, *Naval History Magazine*, 19 (4), August, 2005.https://www.usni.org/magazines/naval-history-magazine/2005/august/navys-barbary-war-crucible.

Dale or Morris. Jefferson was ambivalent about the expeditions because he was concerned about the US being pulled into a European war. He was also concerned about the cost.[72]

During Morris's command of the Mediterranean fleet, the frigate USS *Boston* was on blockade duty outside Tripoli. The American ship joined two Swedish frigates that were also blockading the harbor. On May 16th, 1802, a number of corsairs sallied out from the harbor and were engaged by the blockading frigates. The *Boston* fired several broadsides, and one corsair ship was beached. There were no casualties on the allied ships, and the corsairs' casualties are not known. The *Boston* was soon joined by another American frigate, the *Constellation*, but the Swedes made peace with Tripoli and left for home. This inconclusive action was somehow dignified by the name of the First Battle of Tripoli Harbor.

One thing Morris managed to do was get himself captured by the Tunisians in a separate incident not related to the war with Tripoli. In January 1803, he decided to personally negotiate. He landed, taking along Captain John Rodgers. They and Consul Cathcart met with the pasha. Before the bey allowed the commodore to return to his ship, he demanded the settlement of debts contracted by Consul William Eaton. Morris was the first commodore to be an involuntary guest in the Barbary States. He would not be the last. The bey demanded $22,000 and wanted Eaton removed—he got the $22,000, and Eaton returned to Washington.[73]

In retrospect, it is somewhat surprising that Tunis did not imprison Morris. A US commodore would have been the highest-ranking American hostage Tunis had ever taken. Giving the demanded money and removing Eaton solved the issues, though, and the officers were freed.

In late May and early June, Morris bombarded Tripoli to no effect. He again tried to negotiate directly with Tripoli, offering $10,000 over fifteen years. Yusuf Pasha would have known about the payment to Tunis, and that may have been behind his own extravagant demand of a payment of $200,000 and then $20,000 annually.[74]

---

[72] Fowler, Jr., William. "The Navy's Barbary War Crucible."

[73] Paine, Lincoln. "War is Better Than Tribute."

[74] Paine, Lincoln. "War is Better Than Tribute."

Morris was replaced by Commodore Edward Preble (1761–1807). Preble was yet another US Navy veteran of the American Revolution. He was probably the best commander in the US Navy at that time. He had been captured in action by the Royal Navy and had, like several other US Navy officers, spent time as a prisoner of war, so he knew what it was like to be imprisoned. Preble also had seen service in the Quasi-War, protecting American ships from French privateers in the Gulf and Caribbean. He sailed on the USS Constitution, his flagship. He had been recalled to the US Navy in 1798, along with many other officers, when the US Navy was re-established. Preble had experience at sea and had served for seventeen years as a merchant captain.[75]

Preble was far more aggressive than Dale had been and was far more competent than Morris. He was confident in the power of his ships and the capability of his officers. His first actions did not involve Tripoli. Morocco had become restive. Preble anchored four warships in Tangier, which may or may not have helped smooth things out with Morocco. Consul James Simpson was an able representative, and he and Preble worked well together.[76]

Morocco had actually declared war in February of 1802 in a dispute over shipping and tribute. The dispute was solved in August of that year. Peace with Morocco was important because Morocco's Atlantic ports could affect a significant portion of American trade in the Atlantic. It is not known why, but Morocco was much less intransigent in making agreements with the Americans than the other Barbary States.

The situation Preble had to deal with was that the *Philadelphia* had met with a Moroccan cruiser, the *Mirboka*, which had just captured an American merchant ship days before. Bainbridge, the captain, detained both the cruiser and the captured ship and sent them to Gibraltar. The situation was murky because the Moroccan ship had once belonged to Tripoli and was blockaded in Gibraltar for two years by Americans. The ship had become officially Moroccan by a dubious sale and given

---

[75] Soley, James. "Operations of the Mediterranean Squadron under Commodore Edward Preble, in 1803-04." Proceedings, U.S. Naval Institute, April 1879.
https://www.usni.org/magazines/proceedings/1879/april/operations-mediterranean-squadron-under-commodore-edward-preble.

[76] Huff, Elizabeth. "First Barbary War."

permission to go after American ships by the governor of Tangier.[77]

Negotiation solved the issue. The Americans released the Moroccan ship, the Moroccans released the American ship, the governor of Tangier was censured, and the treaty of 1787 was renewed. With the Moroccan issues resolved, Preble could concentrate on the war with Tripoli. Preble had a highly jaundiced view of the Moroccans and Maghrebians in general, writing to a fellow officer, "The Moors are a deep, designing, artful, treacherous set of villains and nothing will keep them so quiet as a respectable naval force near them."[78]

One action resulted in disaster and was highly embarrassing to the US Navy and the United States. On October 31st, 1803, the frigate *Philadelphia* was on blockade duty outside Tripoli, and lookouts spied a sail. The frigate went to investigate and sailed into dangerous waters in pursuit of the ship. The frigate sailed into water that proved to be too shallow for its size. As a result, it grounded on a sandbar several miles from shore.

Tripoli was quick to notice the grounded frigate and sent gunboats out to capture it. Under several hours of confrontation, the crew made frantic efforts to move the ship, tossing gear over the sides to lighten it, but to no avail. They even drilled holes in the ship's bottom in an attempt to sink her, but the water was too shallow. The captain consulted with his officers to discuss whether to blow the ship up with all hands on board rather than submit to the dishonor of captivity. They decided to surrender. The ship was still armed, although many of the guns were thrown overboard. The remaining guns tilted at such a degree that the guns on one side faced the water and faced the clouds on the other side. The 307 officers and crewmen became prisoners and would spend 20 months in the pasha's prisons.[79]

The captain of the *Philadelphia* was William Bainbridge, the same man who commanded the *George Washington* voyage from Algiers to Istanbul. At sea, the frigate could have blown any ship in Tripoli's fleet out of the water, but aground, faced with enemy guns and a swarm of

---

[77] Soley, James. "Operations of the Mediterranean Squadron under Commodore Edward Preble, in 1803-04."

[78] Soley, James. "Operations of the Mediterranean Squadron under Commodore Edward Preble, in 1803-04."

[79] Boot, Max. *Savage Wars of Peace. Small Wars and the Rise of American Power.* Pg. 18.

small boats, she was helpless.

When Commodore Preble heard about the crew going into captivity, he was angry and wrote, "Would to God that the officers and crew of the *Philadelphia* had one and all determined to prefer death to slavery." The comment means he thought the ship should have blown itself up rather than be dishonored by surrendering. Captain Bainbridge had a different view, saying he never presumed that he had the right to condemn the crew to death.[80]

Preble seems to have been deeply angered about this disaster, but the situation did not change his determination to continue his actions against Tripoli. He arranged for the prisoners to have a clothing allowance and small amounts of money, which were administered through the help of the British consul in the city.[81]

The 307 officers and crewmen captured from the *Philadelphia* gave Tripoli a large number of hostages. When the Tripolitans boarded the frigate, they beat many of the prisoners, pillaged their personal effects, and stripped off their uniforms. The men spent many months in captivity but were restive. Five of them converted to Islam and apparently stayed in the Maghreb the rest of their lives. Two or three died from disease. Most of them petitioned British Admiral Lord Nelson, claiming they were British subjects and asking him to obtain their release. The story is that Nelson said they should all be hanged.[82]

Having over three hundred captives and a powerful ship emboldened Yusuf Pasha. It seemed like he held all the cards. The pasha upped his ransom demands for the captured crew to $3 million, which was equal to a third of the total US federal budget and more than the US spent in total for the Navy, the Army, and all other defense expenditures.

The plight of the crew held prisoner was little better than that of other captives. One prisoner, the *Philadelphia*'s physician, Dr. Jonathan Cowdery, was asked or compelled to help with some very serious illness one of Yusuf's sons was dealing with. Cowdery saved his life, and in return, he was given what amounted to freedom in the city, including

---

[80] Fowler, Jr., William. "The Navy's Barbary War Crucible."

[81] Soley, James. "Operations of the Mediterranean Squadron under Commodore Edward Preble, in 1803-04."

[82] Zeledon, Jason. *The United States and The Barbary Pirates: Adventures in Sexuality, State Building and Nationalism, 1784-1815.* Pg. 140.

writing letters. He was allowed to keep a journal, which has become an important source for historians.[83]

The officers were confined in separate quarters, and their conditions were better. While captives from the crew were made to labor on fortifications and other tasks, the officers obtained books from the Danish consul and set up a prison school with classes in navigation, gunnery, history, and languages.[84]

Despite the inability to subdue Tripoli and the *Philadelphia* disaster, the blockade of Tripoli did have some results. The blockaders captured several Tripolitan ships and also stopped several neutral ships carrying supplies, including a ship loaded with building materials, a Greek ship bound for Tripoli with weaponry that had twenty-five Ottoman soldiers aboard, and a merchant ship carrying six thousand gallons of olive oil.[85]

Preble and the Navy were also involved in devising and supporting an overland army campaign. If they could not blast the harbor enough to bring Yusuf to the peace table, maybe using a family dynastic dispute could overturn him and bring a more pliable pasha to rule Tripoli. Former Consul Eaton and Yusuf's brother became the center of the war.

Yusuf was angry at the continuing blockade. He mulled over having all the prisoners executed, with the exception of Dr. Cowdery. He even threatened to have them burned to death if they plotted with his brother, Hamid.[86]

[83] Sutton, Angela. *White Slaves in Barbary: The Early American Republic, Orientalism and the Barbary Pirates.* Pg. 12.

[84] Wilson, Gary. *American Prisoners in the Barbary Nations, 1784-1816.* Pg. 224.

[85] Zeledon, Jason. *The United States and The Barbary Pirates: Adventures in Sexuality, State Building and Nationalism, 1784-1815.* Pg. 167.

[86] Wilson, Gary. *American Prisoners in the Barbary Nations, 1784-1816.* Pgs. 271-272.

Chapter 4 – War with Tripoli (1804–1805)

The year 1804 marked the most intense fighting of the Barbary Wars, with the Mediterranean squadron blasting away at Tripoli's fortifications, the ships in Tripoli's harbor, and bombarding the city itself several times. Major engagements were fought in the harbor that included Americans swarming aboard Tripolitan gunboats, fighting with cutlasses and rifle butts as if it were the Battle of Lepanto.

By far the most famous exploit of the Barbary Wars and one of the most amazing exploits of any Americans in any war then or since was led by Lieutenant Stephen Decatur. Tripoli's capture of the USS *Philadelphia* threatened to vastly increase the power of their fleet, and the loss of a major American warship to Tripoli was a global embarrassment. Tripoli also had those three hundred prisoners, who could be used as hostages and to demand ransoms.

The frigate was anchored in the harbor, close to shore and under the protection of the guns lining the fortress walls. She was not ready for war because of damage from the grounding, but the Tripolitans were skilled enough at shipbuilding to make the big ship seaworthy once again. The cannons the crew had tossed before capture were salvaged. The masts needed repairs, but the rigging and other needed repairs to get her ready to sail would not have taken long. Her guns were loaded as a precaution.

Commodore Preble decided to risk a raid to neutralize or destroy the frigate. The captured Tripoli ketch that had been renamed the *Intrepid* would be used, and only volunteers would be involved. The ketch had rigging like the typical merchant ships used in the region, which made deception more likely to work. The mission was dangerous and had a low prospect of success and a high prospect of death or being captured. The commodore requested volunteers. Lieutenant Stephen Decatur volunteered, as did seventy sailors.

On the night of February 16th, 1804, the ketch sailed into Tripoli Harbor. Most of the men were concealed below decks, and the men on deck were dressed in Maltese costumes in the hope of looking Maltese and, thus, harmless. Trade between Malta (then a British base) and Tripoli was common, and the ketch looked Mediterranean. The pilot, Salvatore Catalano, was from Malta and knew Arabic. He also knew the harbor, unlike any of the Americans.

It took two hours to reach the frigate. The skeleton crew on board the captured ship was suspicious. The pilot shouted to them that this ketch was a Maltese ship that had lost its anchor and asked for permission to moor alongside the frigate. Permission was granted, and the Tripolitan crew was lulled into thinking the ketch was harmless. It took several minutes for the frigate's crew to realize something was wrong, but the realization came too late, as the Americans swarmed aboard like pirates. They used swords and pistols to clear the Muslim crew, killing many. The rest jumped overboard and swam to shore.[87]

Decatur and his men readied the frigate to be set on fire. Fifteen minutes was enough, and as the Americans reboarded the *Intrepid*, the *Philadelphia* was well on its way to becoming a blazing wreck. The fire burned the anchor cables, and the ship drifted toward shore. As it drifted while on fire, its cannons heated up and began to go off. They had been loaded by the Tripolitan crew as a precaution, and as they went off, the dying ship fired a broadside into the city. The *Philadelphia* then blew up in a spectacular explosion. Equally spectacularly, the *Intrepid* sailed out of the harbor while under fire from the forts, but except for a hole in one sail, it wasn't hit.

No Americans were killed or captured, and any injuries they suffered were minor. The sheer bravado of it caught Tripoli by surprise, and the exploit marked Decatur as a leader. As the story spread, he became famous around the world. British Admiral Nelson expressed his

[87] Boot, Max. *Savage Wars of Peace. Small Wars and the Rise of American Power.* Pg. 4.

admiration for the bravery displayed, and America's embarrassment over losing the frigate vanished.[88]

The prisoners in Tripoli seem to have been as astonished at the exploit as Yusuf Pasha was. Following the event, some of the prisoners were beaten, and conditions became harsher. There were plots to escape. It is not clear why Yusuf did not take out his anger on the group. It would have been like him to have some of them executed. Perhaps he thought they were more valuable alive.

Decatur's miraculous success came at a very opportune moment for President Jefferson. It created a wave of patriotic enthusiasm for the war and for Jefferson at a time when his Federalist opponents were strongly criticizing the war and Jefferson's policies. It erased the defeatist gloom caused by the loss of the *Philadelphia*.[89]

Decatur was also promoted to full captain at the age of twenty-five, which was an extraordinary honor at that time. Captains were generally considerably older and more experienced. This marked him as a man to watch, and as it turned out, Decatur fully lived up to the expectations. Towns in several states were named after him.

One tribute to Decatur's success was a poem written by a Baltimore lawyer named Francis Scott Key, who set his verses to the old English drinking song "To Anacreon in Heaven." After the intense public interest in Decatur's exploit faded, the verses were forgotten. A few years later, Key was a temporary prisoner on a British ship, where he watched the bombardment of Ft. McHenry. Key redid the lyrics, using the same tune, and the result was "The Star-Spangled Banner."[90]

Preble had been authorized to obtain smaller craft to attack Tripoli. The big American frigates drew too much water to chase the nimble corsair ships close to shore. He sailed on the *Constitution* to Naples, the capital of the Kingdom of the Two Sicilies, to request the loan or lease of bomb ketches and gunboats. He was asked to make the request in writing and did so. The king agreed to lend the US six gunboats, two bomb ketches, and six 24-pounder long guns intended for a floating battery. Preble also requested and received supplies of shells, muskets,

[88] Boot, Max. *Savage Wars of Peace. Small Wars and the Rise of American Power.* Pgs. 3-4.

[89] Monsieurs, Roel. *The Causes and Consequences of the First Barbary War 1801-1805.* Pg. 62.

[90] Paine, Lincoln. "War is Better Than Tribute."

sabers, powder and shot, and other supplies.[91]

The Kingdom of the Two Sicilies, which combined Sicily and southern Italy up to Naples, was at war with Tripoli. Naples was periodically at war with various Barbary powers. It was not powerful, and the proximity of Sicily to the North African coast made its coast and shipping very vulnerable to the corsairs. Naples was pleased that Tripoli might be defeated. The Americans made something of a base at Syracuse in Sicily.

The borrowed ships had a shallower draft than the American frigates and could get closer to the city walls. The Neapolitan bomb ketches used a very large piece of artillery called a mortar, which launched a high arching shot. The thirteen-inch mortars were useless in naval combat and were designed more for attacks on fortifications.

The borrowed gunboats and bomb ketches were slow sailing, so Preble had them towed by the faster sailing American ships. The *Constitution* towed several of them, and this was probably the only time American warships towed Italian warships to Africa. The bomb ketches had one big mortar as an armament, and the gunboats usually had one big gun, like a 24-pounder long gun. These gunboats were lateen-rigged and apparently were crewed by ninety-six Sicilians.

Once these reinforcements joined the blockade ships off Tripoli, Preble and his officers planned a bombardment to damage the fortifications and the Tripolitan gunboats and other ships in the harbor. There was never a possibility of an American land assault on Tripoli; the total number of officers, crewmen, and Marines in Preble's force was not much over a thousand, and Tripoli's defenders were estimated at twenty-five thousand. The intent was to inflict enough damage so the pasha would come to the negotiation table, release the prisoners, and agree to stop his corsairs from going after American ships.

The floating battery proved unworkable, so the guns intended for it were temporarily added to the *Constitution*'s already formidable array of cannons.

---

[91] Martin, Tyrone. "Barbary War Bicentennial: Bashing the Bashaw." U.S. Naval Institute, *Naval History Magazine* 18 (4), August 2004. Retrieved April 23, 2003. https://www.usni.org/magazines/naval-history-magazine/2004/august/barbary-war-bicentennial-bashing-bashaw.

In August of 1804, Commodore Preble decided to again attack the gunboats in the harbor. Some of them seemed to be forming up for action, and he seized the opportunity to send in American gunboats (which included the ones borrowed from Sicily) to go after them. The *Constitution* stood by to protect the gunboats with covering fire against the port's land fortifications. It was six American gunboats facing about eighteen Tripolitan gunboats, but the Americans attacked anyway. Decatur led half of the gunboats, and his men boarded two of the enemy ships, engaging in bloody fight after bloody fight. In one of them, thirty-three of the sixty Tripolitan crewmen were killed, with no American losses. Overall, there was one American killed, Lieutenant Decatur, Captain Decatur's brother.[92]

In one part of the fight, nine Americans boarded one of the enemy gunboats, but their own drifted away, so they were left alone on the enemy deck. The nine Americans killed fourteen and captured twenty-two more, capturing the gunboat as well. One of the six American gunboats held back, not engaging with the enemy. Its commander was accused of cowardice.[93]

During the fight, Decatur got the news that his brother had been killed in fighting on another enemy ship, so he led his men against the presumed killers and overwhelmed the gunboat they were on. He got entangled in a literal hand-to-hand fight with the Muslim captain, killing him with a pistol shot. His men captured the gunboat, adding to the other two that had been captured. When they withdrew back to the blockading ships, Decatur reported to Commodore Preble that they had captured three of the enemy gunboats. The story goes that Preble growled, "Where are the rest of them?"[94]

Preble attacked again on August 7th with nine gunboats, which included the three captured in the fight three days earlier. Again, there was hand-to-hand fighting, but this time, there were more American casualties. A hot shot fired from the fort hit one of the captured gunboats and exploded its powder magazine, sinking it and killing nine Americans. This attack inflicted some damage on the Tripolitan corsairs,

[92] Soley, James. "Operations of the Mediterranean Squadron under Commodore Edward Preble, in 1803-04."

[93] Martin, Tyrone. "Barbary War Bicentennial: Bashing the Bashaw."

[94] Boot, Max. *Savage Wars of Peace. Small Wars and the Rise of American Power.* Pgs. 20-21.

and the covering bombardment also inflicted minor damage on the harbor fortifications. The damage was insufficient to bring Yusuf to the bargaining table, though.[95]

Decatur still sought revenge on his brother's killer, which led to another act of legendary heroism. As Decatur was struggling with a burly corsair captain, he was attacked by another Muslim swinging a sword. A sailor named Reuben James interfered and took the blow intended for Decatur, getting a bad slash on his head but almost certainly saving Decatur's life. The sailor later had a warship named after him, the destroyer *Reuben James*, which was sunk in October 1941 by a German U-boat prior to America's involvement in World War II. A sailor did save Decatur, but it might not have been Reuben James. The legend still is considered a classic Navy story. The first gunboat battle is sometimes given the name the Second Battle of Tripoli Harbor.

During this August 7th action, another American ship came into sight. It proved to the USS *John Adams*, which arrived with dispatches from Washington. One of them informed that Decatur was promoted to captain, backdated to the day of his blowing up the *Philadelphia*. At age twenty-five, Decatur's promotion makes him the youngest captain ever appointed in the US Navy, a record that still stands more than two hundred years later.

The *John Adams* also brought other news, some welcome and some not. A substantial reinforcement of US Navy warships was being sent, which was welcome news. The unwelcome news was that there would be a new commander of the Mediterranean squadron, Commodore Samuel Barron. Preble was upset by the news but continued the actions against Tripoli. Barron's assumption of command would not happen until he actually arrived.[96]

The US Navy Department was not replacing Preble because of any fault. Barron was the logical commander to lead the considerable reinforcements being sent to the Mediterranean squadron, and regulations required a senior officer as commander. The Navy operated on seniority based on length of service. If two commanders of the same rank served in the same area, one would have precedence over the

[95] Soley, James. "Operations of the Mediterranean Squadron under Commodore Edward Preble, in 1803-04."

[96] Martin, Tyrone. "Barbary War Bicentennial: Bashing the Bashaw."

other, which would be based on their lengths of service. If one officer had been appointed two or three days earlier than another, the first appointment outranked the slightly later one. Commodore Barron outranked Preble.

On August 28th, Preble tried again. He brought up the gunboats and bomb ketches for a closer bombardment. He moved the *Constitution* within four hundred yards of the fort to engage it and provide cover fire for the bomb ketches and gunboats. This was a risky maneuver, but it worked. The frigate fired nine broadsides at the fort, inflicting some damage. The *Constitution* was a lucky ship; she was hit nineteen times by enemy fire, but the damage was limited to some rigging.[97]

Preble wanted to end Tripoli's intransigent resistance. The commodore badly wanted it to end during his period of command, which might have led to him approving another risky effort. Perhaps he thought that sheer luck would repeat Decatur's amazing results in destroying the *Philadelphia*. Preble and his officers devised another tactic to destroy the many gunboats sheltering in the harbor under the fort's guns. They would again use the *Intrepid*, the ketch that Decatur used to attack the *Philadelphia*, and sail into the harbor loaded with explosives in the hopes of blowing up or setting on fire the Tripolitan gunboat fleet.

The ketch was loaded with a hundred barrels of gunpowder, shells, and other combustibles and was described as an inferno, a name sometimes used for such a ship. It was a variation of the fireship, which had been used for centuries. The idea of a fireship was to load it with combustibles, rig it to sail with the wind at enemy ships by itself with no crew, set it on fire, and release it. Wooden ships were highly vulnerable to fire. Unlike fireships, the *Intrepid* would need a crew because it could not rely on the wind alone. The ketch would tow several boats for the crew to escape in. The plan was for the crew to sail into the harbor under cover of night, light the fuses, abandon ship, and row away in the boats before the fuses ignited the gunpowder.

The mission was more dangerous than the mission to destroy the *Philadelphia* because it added the danger of being blown up by accident to being killed or captured. Still, thirteen sailors volunteered, and they all knew the danger. The ketch was prepared, and on September 4th, the

---

[97] Martin, Tyrone. "Barbary War Bicentennial: Bashing the Bashaw."

men sailed into Tripoli Harbor at night. Preble and the rest watched anxiously for a time, and then a huge explosion lit up the harbor. The *Intrepid* blew up, killing all on board and doing no damage to the enemy ships. It is not known if the explosion was an accident or if the crew blew it up to avoid capture, avoiding the fate of the frigate's crew. The mission's leader was one of the more promising young officers in the US Navy, Master Commander Richard Somers.[98]

Commodore Barron assumed command on September 10th. His reinforcements to the Mediterranean squadron made it more formidable and assured the squadron had the force to continue the war. However, Barron seems to have lacked Preble's aggressive temperament in taking the war to Tripoli.

Preble sailed home aboard the USS *John Adams*, arriving in New York Harbor on February 25th, 1805. He discovered that he was seen as a hero by the people. He dined with Jefferson, Monroe, and other notables. However, his fame faded, and the mission to subdue Tripoli was his last. He never again commanded at sea. He was in poor health and died in 1807.

Commodore Barron was not in the best of health either and spent a portion of his command on land at Syracuse in Sicily, where Preble had established an informal base. Actual command of the squadron was put on Captain John Rodgers while the commodore was ashore. Rodgers was an aggressive and highly competent officer.[99]

Using American superiority at sea had not forced Tripoli to terms. Tripoli had lost gunboats and suffered some damage from bombardment but showed no signs of ending the war. That motivated Barron to approve a bizarre land operation that just might work.

---

[98] Boot, Max. *Savage Wars of Peace. Small Wars and the Rise of American Power*. Pg. 21.

[99] Fowler, Jr., William. "The Navy's Barbary War Crucible."

Chapter 5 – To the Shores of Tripoli (1805)

The most complicated and least understood part of the First Barbary War is the land campaign of 1805, which was led by a former consul to Tunis, William Eaton. It includes a couple of firsts for the United States. It was the first time, as far as it is known, that the United States tried what is today called a "regime change," an attempt to topple a government and replace it with one more friendly. It was the first US military campaign on land invading another nation, other than the American Revolutionary War invasions of Canada, and it was the first US intervention in Africa.

Commodore Barron was frustrated at the ineffectiveness of the efforts to defeat Tripoli. He reluctantly authorized a plan that had been devised by Eaton and discussed in Washington a year or two previously. The plan was to exploit a conflict in the pasha's family and attack Tripoli by land. The scheme resulted in the first overseas land operation in American military history and is the source of the line in the "Marines' Hymn" that says, "From the halls of Montezuma to the shores of Tripoli." Five hundred miles of Tripoli's shores were involved.

Yusuf Karamanli Pasha was a ruthless leader. He was one of three sons of Ali Pasha, who ruled Tripoli for many years. Yusuf was determined to replace his father, and he murdered an older brother and competitor in 1790, shooting him in front of his mother. His father, Ali I Pasha, wanted his remaining son, Hamid, to follow him as ruler. Yusuf disagreed, and the dispute turned violent. Yusuf gathered supporters and besieged Tripoli.

However, an outsider intervened. A Turkish appointee named Ali Burghul and four hundred Greek and Turkish mercenaries captured Tripoli without a shot. Ali I Pasha and his son Hamid found refuge in Tunis while Yusuf besieged the Turkish raiders. Tunis raised an army that is claimed to be twenty thousand strong and marched to Tripoli. The exact nature of the episode is mysterious. If Ali Burghul was sent by the Porte to restore peace, it was foiled. The force plundered the city, and his men left Tripoli after a brief reign of looting and murder. Ali and Hamid returned to their city, and Ali abdicated in favor of Hamid. Hamid (also known as Hamad, Ahmed, and Hamet) lacked Yusuf's determination to rule. In 1794, Hamid left Tripoli for a time, and Yusuf closed the city gates against him, forbidding Hamid to return to the city. Yusuf declared himself the pasha of Tripoli. Yusuf had become popular because of his resistance to Ali Burghul. Hamid had few supporters in the city.[100]

As you can see, the situation in Tripoli was precarious before the First Barbary War even began. The prime mover in a land attack against Tripoli was William Eaton, the former consul in Tunis. Eaton was forty years old and had a checkered history. He had run away to join the US Army at age sixteen, lying about his age to get enrolled, and fought in the American Revolution. He later fought with Mad Anthony Wayne against the Native Americans in the Ohio Country when Wayne broke the power of the tribal alliance at the Battle of Fallen Timbers in 1794. Eaton was accused of misusing US Army funds, for which he was court-martialed and found not guilty. He was appointed American consul to Tunis in 1799, and while in Tunis, he met Hamid. The circumstances of the meeting are not known. Eaton might have learned of this complicated dynastic dispute and decided intervention might be to America's advantage.

A fast and loose manner with government money appears to have been a habit for Eaton. Few details are known about the offense he was court-martialed for, but that was not his last misappropriation of funds. At one point, without authorization, he used $22,000 of official funds to ransom a young European girl from slavery. Jefferson was apparently

---

[100] Paine, Lincoln. "War is Better Than Tribute."

outraged and insisted it be paid back.[101]

Eaton and Cathcart apparently came up with the idea that the dynastic issues between Yusuf and Hamid could be used to America's advantage by installing a friendly ruler in Tripoli who would be grateful for American support and end the war. The idea had been broached as early as 1801 in Washington by Eaton and Cathcart, but it was greeted with caution. Many American politicians were still wary of involvement in a foreign land campaign.[102]

Commodore Barron knew about the plan but was skeptical. He had to be convinced by Eaton and some of his officers. Barron was concerned about the condition of some of his ships after being so long at sea, and the enlistment periods of some of the crews were nearing their end. All the US Navy's bombardments and boarding of gunboats had not dented the pasha's intent to continue the war. The possibility the scheme might quickly topple Yusuf must have strongly appealed to Barron.

The plan involved advancing from Egypt across the Libyan Desert to the coastal city of Derna (also spelled as Darnah), some five hundred miles from Egypt, and capturing that city. Derna was the second-largest town in the regions controlled by Tripoli. Yusuf ruled the hinterland as far as Derna and perhaps beyond. The hope behind Eaton's project was that Hamid's control of Derna would lead to a rise in his popularity in Tripoli. However, Derna was still hundreds of miles from Tripoli.

Yusuf had earlier appointed Hamid to govern Derna. Yusuf apparently was not worried that his brother might use it as a base to recover control of Tripoli. Hamid was poor coup d'état material. The evidence suggests he was a vacillating man with questionable courage.

Hamid played at governing the town but left Derna for Egypt. For unknown reasons, Hamid decided to join the Mamluk rebellion against the Ottomans. So, Eaton had to go to Egypt to find Hamid and discuss a campaign against Derna. It took time to locate him.

In 1805, Egypt was chaotic. The British had defeated the orphaned French Army and repatriated it, but Britain still had forces in the country. Various Mamluk groups were trying to seize power, and the

---

[101] Vivian, Cassandra. "William Eaton: To the Shores of Tripoli." Pg. 69.

[102] Huff, Elizabeth. "First Barbary War."

Ottomans were trying to reestablish authority. Eaton walked into this wildly unstable place and was suspected of being a British spy. He was arrested by an Ottoman figure who had the odd title of the Kerchief of Damanhour. Eaton was briefly imprisoned but somehow was released.[103]

Hamid came to Damanhour to meet him. Eaton managed to extricate both himself and Hamid from the situation in Egypt. He had to persuade the Ottoman authorities that the endeavor was legitimate and did so well enough to obtain permission to recruit a force. How he did so with his limited Arabic can only be imagined. Eaton spoke French, so perhaps he talked their way out of tense situations using that language. He had the reputation of being an extremely persuasive man, and it took all of Eaton's powers of persuasion to keep Hamid involved in the plot.[104]

It seems that Hamid might have gotten cold feet because Eaton apparently had to threaten him with exile in the United States if he did not accept an offer, and other offers and counteroffers seem to have been made.[105]

Eaton knew some Arabic but was not fluent, so he spoke through an interpreter. He imposed a treaty on Hamid. The terms of the agreement specified that once Hamid achieved power in Tripoli, he would order the release of all American prisoners, turn over the tribute from Denmark and Sweden to the US to pay for the costs of the campaign, and turn over Yusuf Pasha and Murad Rais as hostages. Murad Rais was the former Peter Lyle, a deserter of the Royal Navy and the admiral of the Tripolitan fleet.[106]

Eaton was allowed to recruit a force for the expedition to Derna, which was five hundred miles to the west across the Libyan Desert. He hired seventy or so Christian mercenaries, mostly Greeks. The rest of the force, which totaled about seven hundred, included Hamid, several dozens of Hamid's supporters, a few cannoneers, a couple of pieces of artillery, and an assortment of Muslim mercenaries, both Turk and

[103] Vivian, Cassandra. "William Eaton: To the Shores of Tripoli." Pg. 72.

[104] Eller, E. M. "To the Shores of Tripoli." U.S. Naval Institute, Proceedings. *Naval History Magazine* 59 (3) March, 1933. Old series. Retrieved April 20, 2023. https://www.usni.org/magazines/proceedings/1933/march/shores-tripoli.

[105] Folayan, Kola. "Tripoli and the War with the U.S.A, 1801-05." *Journal of African History* 13 (2), 1972. 261-70. JSTOR access April 11, 2023. Pgs. 263-264.

[106] Vivian, Cassandra. "William Eaton: To the Shores of Tripoli." Pg. 29.

Arab. As mentioned, in 1805, Egypt was in turmoil after Napoleon's invasion and fighting over the restoration of Ottoman authority. Alexandria would have had a sizable population of various kinds of unemployed mercenaries, deserters, and adventurers.

The unpromising force had Eaton recruited in command and seven Marines as support. The detachment of seven Marines was provided by the US Navy and commanded by Lieutenant Presley O'Bannon. Eaton had a sort of claim to being in the Army and proclaimed himself to be a general. He probably assumed the title to impress his men rather than having an inflated sense of himself. He proved to have exceptional leadership qualities simply by being able to hold the force together over a five-hundred-mile march in extremely difficult conditions. Apparently, Eaton had wanted to reach Tripoli by sea but was not allowed to find a ship.

Eaton kept a journal of the adventure. It describes his near contempt for the Barbary rulers and something close to contempt for the Arabs in his force, whom he describes as complaining. There was ample reason to complain, as rations grew shorter and shorter, water became equally scarce, and tensions among the groups in the little army rose. Hamid seems to have wanted to turn back. The owners of the camels and horses wanted money upfront, and if they had been so paid, they would probably have deserted during the night. On at least one occasion, Arab mercenaries lined up, ready to attack for more rations, facing off with the Greek Christian mercenaries and the seven Marines in a tense confrontation that lasted several hours. They even had to kill and eat camels, which was always a last resort in the desert.[107]

Eaton's journal is full of references to a variety of problems with the mercenaries. Some of the Arabs threatened to desert, packing up their camels and even leaving, but it turned out to be a kind of acting out rather than actual desertion. At another point, some of the camel drivers wanted more money before moving forward, so Eaton passed the hat around to the non-Arabs and collected $611 to pay them. There were continual problems with too little food and too little water. There were no accurate maps and no roads, only hundreds of miles of coastal desert tracks. Eaton's journals refer to the Bedouins, who had never seen Christians before, and others who investigated the shiny buttons on his

---

[107] Eller, E. M. "To the Shores of Tripoli."

uniform. Eaton seems to have thought of them in terms of savages, something like the Native Americans he had fought in the Ohio Country. He even mentions a mother willing to trade her fourteen-year-old daughter's services for a bag of rice, and he seems to have been tempted.[108]

The Derna campaign must be one of the only times an American commanded a force that was so mixed and was mainly comprised of Muslims. Some of the mercenaries had combat experience, and some seemed to have joined to escape Egypt. The group probably included men from all over the Middle East and Europe. One of the mercenaries claimed to be the illegitimate son of Marie Antoinette's chambermaid.[109]

Eaton seems to have held the army together by sheer force of will. Despite the threats, near starvation, and near violence between Muslim and Christian mercenaries, he moved his men from Alexandria to Derna, more than five hundred miles through the early summer heat and humidity.

The ragtag column wasn't entirely alone. Commodore Barron had detailed three smaller warships to help. These were the sloop *Hornet*, the sloop *Nautilus*, and the brig *Argus*. The sloops carried ten or twelve guns, and the *Argus* carried twenty. Notably, the *Nautilus* was commanded by Oliver Hazard Perry, and both he and the ship would be involved in the War of 1812. Under a different captain, the *Nautilus* fought a British ship in 1812, was captured, and commissioned into the Royal Navy with the same name. Perry supervised the building of and then commanded the Lake Erie fleet that inflicted a decisive defeat on the British at Put-in-Bay in 1813.

Near the end of the march and not far from Derna, the US Navy ships rendezvoused with the force, providing supplies and money for Eaton to pay his mercenaries. The ships had previously waited at the agreed-on point and then sailed away, assuming something had happened to Eaton's army. When the army reached the rendezvous point, no ships were there. Lookouts built fires on high points nearby, and lookouts on the warships saw the smoke, so the warships sailed back to the place, enabling the starving troops to eat and providing money to pay the mercenaries. Eaton seems to have possessed not only charisma

---

[108] Vivian, Cassandra. "William Eaton: To the Shores of Tripoli." Pgs. 80-84.

[109] Boot, Max. *Savage Wars of Peace. Small Wars and the Rise of American Power.* Pg. 24.

but also luck.[110]

As Eaton's army approached its goal, its numbers increased to about 1,200, as some Bedouin tribesmen joined, perhaps sensing an opportunity to do some looting or perhaps as a way to strike back at domination from Tripoli. The tribesmen were with their families, adding even more complexity to the already diverse company. On April 27th, 1805, after briefly resting his force, Eaton attacked Derna, and a battle against far superior numbers lasted for hours. Eaton was facing defeat, so he gambled everything on a wild charge. It won the battle, and Eaton's men broke into the town, routing the defenders.[111]

Eaton's force held Derna for several weeks. Yusuf Pasha reacted quickly and sent a force of about three thousand to attack and recover the town. This force had to cover the several hundred miles between Tripoli and Derna. Yusuf's men attacked three times and were repulsed each time. The defenders were helped by covering fire from the three Navy warships that had shepherded the force in the last part of its march. That support was probably what stymied Yusuf's forces from recapturing Derna. Hamid's supporters fought the forces from Tripoli, and both sides suffered considerable casualties.

While Eaton's force and his seven Marines were fighting on the shores of Tripoli, as the "Marines' Hymn" proclaims, US Consul Tobias Lear was negotiating with Tripoli. It's likely that Eaton's force capturing Derna prompted Yusuf Pasha to want peace. Lear got the *Philadelphia* captives released, presumably minus those who had converted to Islam. They were loaded on American vessels on June 4th. Lear agreed to pay $60,000 in ransom. The agreement effectively ended the war with Tripoli.

Consul Lear had a low opinion of Hamid and did not think the venture could succeed. He was also wary of its possible success, arguing that if Hamid became pasha of Tripoli, he would be a weak ruler and that the US would be drawn in to support his rule.[112]

Eaton found out that a treaty had been agreed to when a message from a US Navy ship reached him. He was ordered to end the campaign and evacuate Derna. There was no way the entire force could be

---

[110] Eller, E. M. "To the Shores of Tripoli."

[111] Folayan, Kola. "Tripoli and the War with the U.S.A, 1801-05." Pg. 264.

[112] Wilson, Gary. *American Prisoners in the Barbary Nations, 1784-1816.*

evacuated, so Eaton decided to leave under cover of darkness. On the night of June 12th, Eaton, the Marines, Hamid, and a few of his supporters rowed out to the *Constellation*. The seventy or so Christian mercenaries and the artillerists were also taken aboard. Apparently, as the last of them were boarding, hundreds of those left behind were on the beach, begging to be taken away. It was a dishonorable end to a remarkable, if troubled, expedition.[113]

Eaton was disgusted at abandoning the force and the town but followed orders. What happened to the hundreds of mercenaries left behind is not known, but their fates were probably grim. Eaton, Hamid, and the rest were taken to Syracuse. Hamid returned to Egypt and never again was a threat to his brother, Yusuf. What happened to the rest of the men taken to Syracuse is not known.

If Eaton had not been called off, his plan seems to have been to continue marching on to Tripoli. He might have hoped for an uprising in Tripoli in favor of Hamid. However, Yusuf was a formidable leader and could put together a considerable force. He put down Arab revolts in the interior in 1802 and 1803 with 1,500 mercenaries and 12,000 cavalrymen. The European consuls believed Yusuf could field as many as thirty thousand infantry and twenty thousand cavalry. Even with Eaton's drive and ability, it would have been difficult to overcome those odds.[114]

Lear negotiated a secret clause with Yusuf, which allowed Yusuf to take up to four years to return Hamid's family, whom Yusuf had earlier taken hostage. The secret clause essentially meant Hamid's family continued to be held hostage for those years. It is not clear if the US Senate would have ratified the treaty if they had been aware of that secret clause. But as it was, the Senate ratified the treaty with Tripoli on April 3rd, 1806.[115]

Later in 1805, the Ottoman appointee to govern Egypt took control. Muhammad Ali, who was from Albania, ruled Egypt from 1805 to 1848. He solved the problem of the rebellious Mamluks by massacring them. His dynasty lasted until 1952. His Egypt eventually expanded to rule much of Sudan, some of Arabia, and Palestine and came very close to

---

[113] Eller, E. M. "To the Shores of Tripoli."

[114] Folayan, Kola. "Tripoli and the War with the U.S.A, 1801-05." Pg. 269.

[115] Huff, Elizabeth. "First Barbary War."

overturning the Ottomans and perhaps becoming sultan himself. Whether Muhammad Ali had any involvement in Eaton's adventure or with Hamid is not known.

Yusuf remained pasha of Tripoli for many years after the Barbary Wars, maintaining his rule until 1832, when he abdicated in favor of his son, Ali. He died in 1836 at the age of seventy-two, an unusually ripe old age for a Barbary Coast ruler. Civil war broke out among three of his sons, and the Ottomans returned in force, ostensibly to restore order, but they took control, deposing Ali II. Tripoli remained Ottoman until the Italians seized it in 1911.

William Eaton was disgusted at what he saw as the betrayal of Hamid. He returned to the US and dabbled in politics in Massachusetts. He seems to have become a heavy drinker and died in 1811, possibly from alcoholism.[116]

Hamid returned to Egypt and seems to have spent the rest of his life there.

[116] Vivian, Cassandra. "William Eaton: To the Shores of Tripoli." Pg. 83.

Chapter 6 – The Second Barbary War (1815)

The sizable increase in the US Navy and the experience of its commanders were useful in another war. The First Barbary War served as a training ground for seamen and officers who led important events in the War of 1812 and in routine cruises against pirates. Between 1805 and 1810, the US Navy stationed several gunboats in newly acquired New Orleans under Captain Joshua Shaw and Master Commandant David Porter. They patrolled and protected American shipping in the Gulf and the Caribbean from French and Spanish privateers, who were not so different from the Muslim corsairs an ocean away.[117]

Many veterans of the Barbary War served admirably during the War of 1812. Stephen Decatur was probably the most notable among them. While captain of the frigate *United States*, Decatur met up with the HMS *Macedonian* near the Azores in October 1812 and emerged the winner in a hard-fought duel between frigates. The British ship was a fifth-rate, 38-gun frigate and was outgunned by the heavy American ship and plainly out-commanded. The *Macedonian* was repaired and incorporated into the US Navy.

---

[117] Grimmet, Richard. "Instances of Use of United States Armed Forces Abroad, 1798-2000." Washington, D.C. Library of Congress, 2002. Retrieved April 13, 2023. https://apps.dtic.mil/sti/pdfs/ADA463153.pdf.

There's a story that both frigates were docked near each other in 1810, and the British captain bet Decatur a beaver hat that if the two ships ever met in combat, the *Macedonian* would win. There's no evidence that the defeated British captain provided the hat. It was, however, typical of the several frigate-to-frigate combats in the war for the winner to refuse to accept the sword of the defeated captain as an acknowledgment of the defeated captain's courage. That kind of gesture was unknown between European ships and Barbary ships.

Later in the war, Decatur captained another frigate, the *President*, with less favorable results. In January 1815, Decatur sailed his frigate into the Atlantic, past the British blockade, but then encountered a strong British squadron and finally got into a running fight with the Royal Navy frigate *Endymion*. Both ships were damaged and suffered severe casualties, but other ships in the squadron were bearing down, so Decatur struck his flag and surrendered the ship to the vastly superior force. Decatur was imprisoned in Bermuda (then a British base) and released when the war ended. The *President* was repaired and entered the Royal Navy as the HMS *President*.

Another Barbary Coast veteran, William Bainbridge, became captain of the *Constitution*. While on patrol seeking to capture and disrupt British shipping, he met with the British frigate *Java* off the coast of Brazil. In a hard-fought duel between the two frigates, *Java* was turned into a wreck and surrendered. The damage was so bad that the ship was burned. Its crewmen transferred to the *Constitution* and were then taken to the Brazilian port of Bahia. Bainbridge had surrendered to a French warship in the Quasi-War, commanded *George Washington* on its notorious harem and zoo voyage, and then commanded the *Philadelphia* when it was lost at Tripoli. His luck had finally turned.

The War of 1812 was vastly greater in scale than the Barbary Wars, and its impact on American shipping was also far larger. There were about 500 American privateers who took somewhere between 1,100 and 1,300 British merchant ships, with close to 400 of those ships being recaptured by the British. The British seized about 1,400 American merchant ships. Estimates of these numbers vary, but there is no doubt they dwarfed the number of ships taken by the Barbary corsairs.

Algiers was impatient with America's slowness to pay tribute. In 1807, the tribute was two years behind. Its corsairs captured a couple of American ships. One of them, the *Mary Ann*, which was captured in

1807, has an unusual ending. After her capture, a prize crew of eight Algerian sailors and a boy was put on board to sail it back to Tripoli. The American crew broke loose, went up on deck, and overcame their captors. They threw four of the men overboard and put the other four Algerians in a boat, cast it adrift, and then sailed on. They did not harm the boy.[118]

Algerine corsairs also captured two other ships. Both ships and their crews were released when the American consul paid the overdue money.

In July of 1812, a few weeks after the US declared war on Britain, the dey of Algiers, Hadji Ali, informed the American consul that the quality of naval stores that had been delivered as part of the agreed upon tribute was not acceptable. He demanded $27,000 instead. The consul, Tobias Lear, disagreed, but Hadji Ali insisted. Lear borrowed the money and made the payment (consuls had considerable leeway to make such arrangements). Lear left in late July. Algiers then declared war, and in August, corsairs captured the American brig *Edwin*, along with its captain and ten-man crew.[119]

The British gave tacit support to Algiers, sending the dey formal letters saying that Britain supported actions by Algiers if those actions were directed at Britain's enemies, a clear reference to the US. There was not much American commerce left for the Algerian corsairs to attack, though, because, between British privateers and the Royal Navy, Americans were swept off the seas.

Negotiations could still take place. American consuls in the other Barbary States could bargain with Algiers. There were also American merchants residing in Europe. In 1813, one of them, a resident in Spain, assumed the identity of a Spaniard and traveled to Algiers in an attempt to make a deal to free American captives. However, it was a non-starter, and the dey was not interested.[120]

The year 1815 saw the French menace end, so the British became unconcerned with neutral ships trading with the French. There was a brief and closely run renaissance of Napoleon when he returned to France from exile in Elba, but his comeback was forever ended with his

---

[118] Wilson, Gary. *American Prisoners in the Barbary Nations, 1784-1816.* Pg. 291.

[119] Lambert, Frank. *The Barbary Wars. American Independence in the Atlantic World.* New York: Hill and Wang, 2005. Pgs. 183-184.

[120] Lambert, Frank. *The Barbary Wars. American Independence in the Atlantic World.* Pg. 189.

defeat at Waterloo on June 18th, 1815. The end of the Napoleonic Wars and the end of the War of 1812 meant that the British no longer needed to stop American ships and impress sailors to man British warships. This removed the two main issues between Britain and the US and opened up the Atlantic for an American expedition to Algiers.

President James Madison was concerned about the continuing threat from Algiers to American trade. Peace in Europe and the end of the war with Britain saw a sharp increase in trade. On March 3rd, 1815, Congress authorized military action against Algiers.

The command of the force was given to the hero of the First Barbary War, Commodore Stephen Decatur. The rank of admiral did not yet exist in the US Navy, or Decatur would have attained that rank. Decatur had a rather strong force, including his flagship, the new 44-gun *Guerriere*, as well as the *Macedonian*, the *Constellation*, and others. With the end of the War of 1812, it became possible for American warships to visit and resupply at ports like Gibraltar and Malta.

Decatur's squadron reached Gibraltar after a rather fast passage. In an action-filled few days, the squadron dealt with some formidable corsairs and appeared before Algiers on June 28th, 1815, only thirty-nine days after the squadron had sailed from New York.[121]

There was some fighting at sea before they reached Algiers, in which the US Navy excelled. On June 17th, 1815, Decatur sighted the Algerian 44-gun frigate *Mashouda* and pursued it. The *Guerriere* fired two broadsides into the enemy, and the Algerian crew ran below deck, making as if to surrender. The initial surrender was a ruse, as the ship then tried to escape, but it was chased and caught by the American ship *Epervier*, an 18-gun brig. The *Epervier* fired five broadsides at the Algerian ship, which then surrendered. Decatur put a prize crew on board and sent the *Mashouda* into Cartagena, Spain, as a prize, along with 406 prisoners.[122]

No Americans were killed by enemy fire, but there was one gory accident on board an American frigate. A cannon exploded, killing five sailors and seriously injuring thirty more. Cannons bursting aboard ships were infrequent but devastating. It occurred because of jams in the ammunition, accidents with loading gunpowder and shot, metal fatigue in

[121] Lambert, Frank. *The Barbary Wars. American Independence in the Atlantic World.* Pg. 142.

[122] Daughan, George. *1812, The Navy's War.* New York: Basic Books, 2011. Pg. 407.

the barrel, and when a cannon was loaded twice by mistake.

Days later, on June 19th, Decatur caught and captured another Algerian ship, the 22-gun brig *Estedio*. The brig tried to escape into shallower water but was cut off by the small ships in Decatur's squadron. Again, a prize crew was put aboard and sailed the captured ship and crew to Cartagena. Capturing the two ships and having almost five hundred prisoners gave Decatur useful bargaining chips and was a wake-up call that the Algerian fleet was outgunned.

The frigate and the brig were the most powerful units in the Algerian fleet and seemed to have brought the dey to his senses, as he realized that he was in danger of defeat. The encounter with the *Mashouda* was called the Battle off Cape Gata, and the encounter with the *Estedio* was called the Battle of Cape Palas.

As mentioned, on June 28th, 1815, Decatur and some of his squadron sailed into the harbor of Algiers. Hadji Ali was murdered in 1814 and was replaced by a man who was murdered six weeks later. The new dey was Omar. The rule of Algiers was notably violent. From 1671 to 1830, twenty-seven deys ruled the city, and fourteen of them achieved power following the murder of their predecessor. Regardless of the power struggles, Decatur insisted on a fast agreement and threatened to continue the war if one was not forthcoming.[123]

The Swedish consul helped the dey negotiate and pointed out to Decatur that Omar was not the dey who declared war. In the resulting agreement, which was completed in a matter of hours, Algiers agreed to permanently give up requests for tribute and cease troubling American shipping. Algiers released ten American captives, and as a gesture of goodwill, Decatur ordered the two captured ships and the five hundred prisoners at Cartagena to be released. The agreement allowed presents to be made but ended the tribute.[124]

A tragic sidebar to the war was the USS *Epervier*. There were ten Americans in captivity in Algiers who were released by the agreement. Decatur had the prisoners board the *Epervier*, which he tasked with returning to New York with the freed prisoners and dispatches describing the victory. He also sent home two officers who had recently

---

[123] Wilson, Gary. *American Prisoners in the Barbary Nations, 1784-1816*. Pg. 4.

[124] Lambert, Frank. *The Barbary Wars. American Independence in the Atlantic World*. Pgs. 191-192.

married and wanted to return home to be with their new families. The *Epervier* had been a Royal Navy ship until it was captured in an 1814 engagement with the USS *Peacock*. It had been repaired and commissioned into the US Navy. She was an unlucky ship. On her way back to New York, she disappeared, and the men on board were never heard from again. It is likely they all drowned in a storm.[125]

Decatur and his fleet sailed to Tunis on July 25th, 1815, with three frigates and three smaller ships. The US was not at war with Tunis, but Decatur seems to have been determined to awe all of the Barbary States. One issue was that two prizes taken by an American privateer during the War of 1812 had been anchored at Tunis but had been recaptured by a British warship. Decatur demanded forty-six thousand Spanish dollars as reparations. The Spanish dollar had long been the currency of choice in Mediterranean trade on account of the purity of its silver content. Tunis paid up.

The fleet sailed to Tripoli, reaching it on August 5th. There was another issue with two more prizes of an American privateer that Tripoli had allowed a British warship to recapture. Decatur demanded money and got twenty-five Spanish dollars and the release of ten Christian captives, eight Sicilians, and two Danes.

The decisive action by the Mediterranean squadron impressed people, although the British were too busy with the aftermath of Waterloo to pay much attention. It was also a boost for Americans. According to one account, when the American squadron anchored at Gibraltar, it fired a seventeen-gun salute. Gibraltar responded with a fifteen-gun salute. An American officer was immediately rowed ashore, where he said the American force expected its salute to be returned gun for gun. He demanded that two more guns be fired to make the salutes equal, and the British governor of Gibraltar complied. Salutes were common and formed a kind of military etiquette.[126]

If that story is true, then it marks a significant improvement in the US Navy's status. The United States was still a junior power among the major powers at the time (at sea, those were Britain and France), but salutes like that were a recognition that a country deserved respect. It would have meant less from Algiers, where the American force had

[125] Daughan, George. *1812, The Navy's War*. New York: Basic Books, 2011. Pg. 408.

[126] Lambert, Frank. *The Barbary Wars. American Independence in the Atlantic World*. Pg. 196.

overwhelmed them, but from Britain, it was significant.

Decatur was informed that he was being relieved by an incoming American squadron and commander, Bainbridge, so he sent the bulk of the squadron to rendezvous with them. He sailed on the *Guerriere* to Gibraltar. On the way, he passed an Algerian fleet consisting of four frigates and three sloops. Decatur readied his ship for action, but no one fired a shot. Famously, the Algerian admiral shouted through a speaking trumpet, "Where are you going?" and Decatur responded, "Anywhere I want to!"[127]

Decatur arrived back in New York on November 12th, with the rest of the force putting into Newport, Rhode Island, a couple of weeks later. Decatur received another hero's welcome. The country was in a buoyant mood because earlier in the year, Andrew Jackson's collection of Tennessee militiamen, freed slaves, and pirates had nearly destroyed a British invasion force at the Battle of New Orleans, inflicting two thousand casualties for the loss of under a hundred Americans.

Commodore Bainbridge arrived in Cartagena, Spain, in September 1815. The USS *Independence*, his flagship, was especially notable since it was the US Navy's first ship of the line, a 74-gun ship. The fact Congress chose to invest in such a large and formidable ship meant that American politicians were no longer wary of a professional navy and saw a formidable force as a good investment. That change was bought about by hard campaigning against the Barbary pirates and by the spectacular performance of American frigates against Royal Navy frigates in the War of 1812.

President Madison ordered the US Navy to maintain a patrol in the Mediterranean as insurance against the Barbary corsairs. The Navy sent the frigates *Constellation*, the *United States*, and two sloops to maintain an American presence there.[128]

---

[127] Daughan, George. *1812, The Navy's War*. New York: Basic Books, 2011. Pg. 409.

[128] Lambert, Frank. *The Barbary Wars. American Independence in the Atlantic World*. Pg. 197.

Conclusion

The First Barbary War was the longest US war besides the American Revolution and the Vietnam War. It was seven weeks longer than the Civil War and four months longer than American involvement in World War 2.[129]

It was the first war that saw American involvement in the Mediterranean and, with the exception of a few American Revolutionary War operations like John Paul Jones's raids on England, was the first American war in the Old World.

The First Barbary War saw a large expansion of the US Navy. It went from a small service with little renown to a fairly large and internationally respected force. Between 1793 and 1807, the US Navy commissioned the construction of thirteen frigates of twenty-eight to forty-four guns each, five brigs of eight to eighteen guns, four schooners of ten to twelve guns, three sloops of ten to twenty-four guns, and an assortment of gunboats and bomb ketches.[130]

The workhorses of the US Navy were those frigates. Again and again, they proved exceptionally powerful. They established the Navy's reputation for being a formidable and generally well-commanded force. In the War of 1812, they did far better than expected, stunning the Royal Navy, with the Americans winning several frigate-to-frigate duels. After the end of the war, the US Navy began constructing more ships,

---

[129] Paine, Lincoln. "War is Better Than Tribute."

[130] Monsieurs, Roel. *The Causes and Consequences of the First Barbary War 1801-1805.* Pg. 25.

including the country's first 74-gun ship of the line. However, the really big ships didn't turn out to be particularly useful, so the frigates remained the most useful.

Following the end of the Second Barbary War, the US had no more trouble with piracy in the Mediterranean. The major naval force sent to combat Algiers in 1815 was sufficient enough to establish the United States as a significant naval power. There has been a US naval presence in the Mediterranean ever since.

The brief Second Barbary War solved the problem of Barbary corsairs preying on American shipping. However, it did not eliminate the need to protect American merchant ships from piracy elsewhere. Between 1815 and 1823, there were more than three thousand pirate and privateer attacks in the Caribbean. The US Navy also allied with the British in conducting anti-slaving patrols off the West African coast, although American participation was spotting and not well supported by Congress. Americans also cooperated with the British in fighting piracy off the Chinese coast.

In 1822, Commodore James Biddle commanded a squadron of two frigates, four sloops, two brigs, four schooners, and two gunboats in the West Indies, an indication of the seriousness of the problem and as large as the forces sent against the Barbary corsairs.[131]

Commodore Biddle was a veteran of the Barbary Wars and had been captured when the Philadelphia surrendered. He spent eighteen months as a captive in prison in Tripoli, which likely biased him against pirates and privateers. The Gulf of Mexico and the Caribbean Sea seethed with pirates and privateers during and after the Napoleonic Wars (1803–1815). The fight for independence from Spain and competing leadership factions also led to maritime chaos. Hundreds of ships were given privateering licenses, which, in theory, allowed them to attack ships flying the enemy flag, but continual uncertainty about who was the enemy was a convenient excuse for piracy.

The First Barbary War served as a warm-up for the US Navy since the War of 1812 would soon follow. The fate of the commanders involved in the Barbary Wars participating in the War of 1812 was mixed. Some of them served with great distinction during the War of 1812, especially Decatur. Oliver Hazard Perry won the crucial Battle of

---

[131] Grimmet, Richard. "Instances of Use of United States Armed Forces Abroad, 1798-2000."

Lake Erie, and Thomas Macdonough won the equally important Battle of Lake Champlain. Those two battles stopped a full British invasion and assured control of the Ohio Country, which more than made up for the losses of ships on the oceans. Other officers achieved important victories as well. Isaac Hull commanded the *Constitution* in its victorious duel with the HMS *Guerriere* in 1812, Decatur and the *United States* defeated the *Macedonian* in 1812, and later in that same year, Bainbridge and the *Constitution* (which had changed captains) defeated the *Java*.

The greatest hero of the Barbary Wars and the commander during the Second Barbary War was Stephen Decatur. His remarkable career came to a sad and miserable end. Decatur presided over the Navy Board of Inquiry over the behavior of Captain James Barron, commander of the USS *Chesapeake*, in an infamous incident. The *Chesapeake* was hailed by the HMS *Leopard* in 1807. James Barron was the brother of Commodore Samuel Barron, who commanded the Mediterranean squadron at the end of the First Barbary War. James Barron also served in the wars, and their names have sometimes been confused.

The captain of the *Leopard*, a British ship of the line, wanted to check the American frigate for British deserters, and when Barron refused, it opened fire. The *Chesapeake* struck its flag after firing one shot. British officers then boarded the frigate and seized several men they accused of desertion. The men seized were charged with desertion, and one of them was later hanged. The incident outraged the American public, and a war nearly broke out. Barron was heavily criticized for yielding his ship, and accusations of cowardice were made. His decision was rational in the sense that a 38-gun frigate would probably have been destroyed by a 74-gun ship. It was the same kind of decision that Bainbridge made by not blowing up the *Philadelphia* in Tripoli.

Barron was court-martialed and suspended from command for five years without pay. The captain was angry over the result and carried a grudge against Decatur. Barron spent several years in Europe and returned home. He was angered by some of Decatur's remarks reported in the press and challenged him to a duel, a common event among Navy officers since they were touchy about their reputations. They met for a duel on March 22nd, 1820, at a dueling ground in Maryland. Both men were hit, but Decatur died from his wounds that night while Barron eventually recovered.[132]

The fates of the Barbary States varied. Most of Europe's diplomats gathered together in Vienna after the final defeat of Napoleon. Called the Congress of Vienna, it set the terms for peace after the long Napoleonic Wars. One thing the Congress of Vienna did was condemn Barbary slavery.[133]

In an incident during 1816, two hundred Italian fishermen under the protection of the British were murdered by Algerian corsairs, an incident that greatly angered the British. In 1816, a combined British and Dutch fleet attacked Algiers, bombarding it for nine hours, heavily damaging the city and killing thousands of its residents. Algiers surrendered and was forced to end its corsair ways. The dey was forced to release all the European captives, about 1,650 of them (estimates vary). This was the effective end of the Barbary pirates once and for all.[134]

Algiers was taken by the French in 1830, and a colonial regime was imposed on the city and its hinterland in a long and ruthless war. Algeria was eventually incorporated into the French colonial empire, and unlike the other African colonies, it was heavily colonized by European settlers, especially from Malta, Italy, and Spain. It could be seen as a reversal of the centuries of corsairs plundering the Mediterranean coasts of Europe. Ultimately, Algeria became an independent nation after a prolonged war of independence.

Tunis maintained a shadowy independence until 1881 when it was incorporated into the French African empire. Tunisia was a protectorate rather than a colony. In theory, the Tunisians had a kind of home rule, and the colonial regime was more respectful of Islam in Tunis than in other places.

Tripoli was reincorporated into the Ottoman Empire in the 1830s and faded into a backwater port of a neglected province. The Ottomans never regained control of Egypt, which prospered under a dynasty descended from an Ottoman governor of Albanian origin. Tripoli became Italian in 1911 as booty from the Italo-Turkish War of 1911-12.

---

[132] Boot, Max. *Savage Wars of Peace. Small Wars and the Rise of American Power.* Pg. 29.

[133] Ribiero, Jorge Martins. "Conflict and Peace in the Mediterranean: Barbary Privateering in the Late 18th and Early 19th Centuries." Pg. 166.

[134] Zeledon, Jason. *The United States and The Barbary Pirates: Adventures in Sexuality, State Building and Nationalism, 1784-1815.* Pg. 368.

The city remained connected to the ancient trade across the Sahara that involved salt, slaves, and gold, although that trade also faded into a shadow of itself. That trade finally became extinct when Africa was carved up into European colonies after the infamous Congress of Berlin.

Morocco remained independent until 1912 when France forced the sultan to cede sovereignty. The former Barbary Coast from Morocco to Tunis came under French rule, with Tripoli and Cyrenaica under Italian rule. The entire Barbary Coast region from Morocco to the borders of Egypt became involuntarily part of a much greater and bloodier war in World War 2.

The two Barbary Wars have been largely forgotten by most Americans, just like the Quasi-War with France a couple of years before. "The shores of Tripoli" is still part of the "Marines' Hymn," although most people who sing the lyrics probably do not understand the reference. Few Americans, except Middle Eastern specialists, are aware that the first American involvement in a land war overseas was in what is now Libya.

The centuries of Barbary slave raiding have become part of the contemporary debate over the place of slavery in American history. Some observers point to the centuries of slavery of white Europeans by Africans and equate it with the slavery of Africans in the centuries of the Atlantic slave trade. That debate tends to forget that the Barbary slavers were North Africans and that the trade was far smaller than the Atlantic trade. It also does not factor in the number of Catholic orders dedicated to rescuing enslaved Christians, which pulled tens of thousands of captives from enslavement, something that would have been impossible to do in the Atlantic trade.

Here's another book by Captivating History that you might like

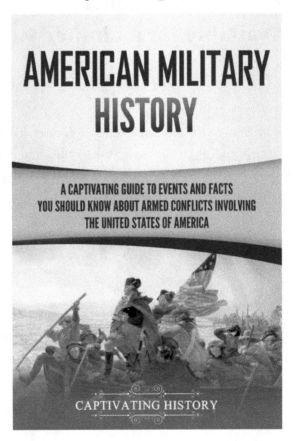

Free Bonus from Captivating History (Available for a Limited time)

Hi History Lovers!

Now you have a chance to join our exclusive history list so you can get your first history ebook for free as well as discounts and a potential to get more history books for free! Simply visit the link below to join.

Captivatinghistory.com/ebook

Also, make sure to follow us on Facebook, Twitter and Youtube by searching for Captivating History.

Works Cited

Baepler, Paul. "White Slaves, African Masters." *Annals of the American Association of Political and Social Science.* Vol. 588, July 2003. 90-111. JSTOR access, April 11, 2023.

Boot, Max. *Savage Wars of Peace. Small Wars and the Rise of American Power.* New York: Basic Books, 2002.

Daly, Robert. The Diplomatic Relations of the United States with the Barbary Coast, 1790-1801. Thesis, Loyola University, Chicago, IL., 1940 https://ecommons.luc.edu/cgi/viewcontent.cgi?referer=&httpsredir=1&article=1 128&context=luc_theses

Davies, J. D. "The Barbary Corsair Raid on Iceland, 1627." Blog. https://jddavies.com/2017/02/20/the-barbary-corsair-raid-on-iceland-1627/

Daughan, George. *1812, The Navy's War.* New York: Basic Books, 2011.

Eller, E. M. "To the Shores of Tripoli." U.S. Naval Institute, Proceedings. *Naval History Magazine* 59 (3) March, 1933. Old series. Retrieved April 20, 2023. https://www.usni.org/magazines/proceedings/1933/march/shores-tripoli.

Folayan, Kola. "Tripoli and the War with the U.S.A, 1801-05." *Journal of African History* 13 (2), 1972. 261-70. JSTOR access April 11, 2023.

Fowler, Jr., William. "The Navy's Barbary War Crucible." U.S. Naval Institute, *Naval History Magazine,* 19 (4), August, 2005.https://www.usni.org/magazines/naval-history-magazine/2005/august/navys-barbary-war-crucible.

Grimmet, Richard. "Instances of Use of United States Armed Forces Abroad, 1798-2000." Washington, D.C. Library of Congress, 2002. Retrieved April 13, 2023. https://apps.dtic.mil/sti/pdfs/ADA463153.pdf.

Huff, Elizabeth. "First Barbary War." August, 2011. *Thomas Jefferson*

Encyclopedia. Retrieved April 13, 2023. https://www.monticello.org/research-education/thomas-jefferson-encyclopedia/first-barbary-war/.

Jamieson, Alan. *Lords of the Sea. A History of the Barbary Corsairs.* London: Reaktion Books, 2012.

Johnson, Ben. "Barbary Pirates and English Slaves." History UK. Retrieved April 11, 2023. https://www.historic-uk.com/HistoryUK/HistoryofEngland/Barbary-Pirates-English-Slaves/

Kitzen, Michael. "Money Bags and Cannon Balls: The Origin of the Tripolitan War, 1795-1801." Journal of the Early Republic 16 (4), Winter 1996. 601-24. JSTOR access, April 11, 2023.

Lambert, Frank. *The Barbary Wars. American Independence in the Atlantic World.* New York: Hill and Wang, 2005.

Lazerowitz, Evan. "America's Second War of Independence: The Barbary Pirate Wars and their Effect on American Geopolitical Power." Georgetown University Law Center, Washington, D.C. December 4, 2008. 1-15. Retrieved April, 2023. https://papers.ssrn.com/sol3/papers.cfm?abstract_id=1955322.

Martin, Tyrone. "Barbary War Bicentennial: Bashing the Bashaw." U.S. Naval Institute, *Naval History Magazine* 18 (4), August 2004. Retrieved April 23, 2003. https://www.usni.org/magazines/naval-history-magazine/2004/august/barbary-war-bicentennial-bashing-bashaw.

Meredith, Martin. *The Futures of Africa,* New York: Public Affairs, 2014.

Monsieurs, Roel. *The Causes and Consequences of the First Barbary War 1801-1805.* Thesis, July 2016. Erasmus University, Rotterdam, NE. Retrieved April 9, 2023. https://thesis.eur.nl/pub/34940

Paine, Lincoln. "War is Better Than Tribute." U.S. Naval Institute, *Naval History Magazine* 15 (3), June 2001. Retrieved April 1, 2023. https://www.usni.org/magazines/naval-history-magazine/2001/june/war-better-tribute.

Prom, William. "The Seventh Frigate." *Naval History Magazine* 34 (4), April 17, 2020. Retrieved April 17, 2023. https://www.usni.org/magazines/naval-history-magazine/2020/august/seventh-frigate.

Rejeb, Lotfi ben. Review of The End of Barbary Terror, Frederick Leisner. *Social History,* XLI (82), November 2008. 629-31. Retrieved April 9, 2023. https://core.ac.uk/download/pdf/268421766.pdf

Ribiero, Jorge Martins. "Conflict and Peace in the Mediterranean: Barbary Privateering in the Late 18th and Early 19th Centuries." 159-179 in D'Angelo and Ribiero, Editors, *Borders and Conflicts in the Mediterranean.* Fisciano, Italy 2016. Retrieved April 13, 2023. https://repositorio-aberto.up.pt/bitstream/10216/86826/2/163741.pdf

Soley, James. "Operations of the Mediterranean Squadron under Commodore Edward Preble, in 1803-04." Proceedings, U.S. Naval Institute, April 1879. https://www.usni.org/magazines/proceedings/1879/april/operations-mediterranean-squadron-under-commodore-edward-preble.

Sutton, Angela. *White Slaves in Barbary: The Early American Republic, Orientalism and the Barbary Pirates.* Thesis, Vanderbilt University, Nashville, TN, 2009. Retrieved April 10, 2023. https://ir.vanderbilt.edu/xmlui/bitstream/handle/1803/14312/SuttonWhiteSlaves.pdf?sequence=1&isAllowed=y

Tinniswood, Adrian. *Pirates of Barbary,* New York: Riverhead Books, 2010. Google Books access April 13, 2023. https://www.google.com/books/edition/Pirates_of_Barbary/IBSVMivndEQC?hl=en&gbpv=1&dq=History+Barbary+States&printsec=frontcover

U.S.S. Constitution Museum. "The Quasi-War with France (1798-1801)." https://ussconstitutionmuseum.org/major-events/the-quasi-war-with-france/.

Vivian, Cassandra. "William Eaton: To the Shores of Tripoli." Academia.edu. Retrieved April 20, 2023. https://www.academia.edu/17964588/William_Eaton_To_the_Shores_of_Tripoli.

Wilson, Gary. *American Prisoners in the Barbary Nations,* 1784-1816. Dissertation, North Texas State University, 1979. https://digital.library.unt.edu/ark:/67531/metadc331824/m2/1/high_res_d/1002783548-Wilson.pdf

Zeledon, Jason. *The United States and The Barbary Pirates: Adventures in Sexuality, State Building and Nationalism, 1784-1815.* Dissertation, University of California, Santa Barbara, 2016. Retrieved April 11, 2023. https://www.alexandria.ucsb.edu/lib/ark:/48907/f3qj7hcm.

Printed in the USA
CPSIA information can be obtained
at www.ICGtesting.com
LVHW021824091123
763047LV00110B/148